THE CYCLE OF
BITCOIN PROFIT

THE CYCLE OF BITCOIN PROFIT

THE BREAKOUT PLAYBOOK FOR CRYPTO
TRADING, MANAGING RISKS &
ACCUMULATING WEALTH

NYCE AYUK

ACKNOWLEDGEMENT

To my dad who loved and helped others unconditionally and showed me to do same for humanity. I am eternally grateful to him.

And to you, crypto traders and investors working your socks off daily, cheers to your big break.

CONTENTS

PREFACE

The book, 'The Cycle of Bitcoin Profit' has laid bare crypto currency cycle in your own best interest; it shows you how you can leverage crypto narratives and the practical steps you need to take to create wealth within the crypto ecosystem.

The major pointers to wealth creation poignantly exposed in this book include: strategies you need to create wealth through flipping coins for profit, a veteran's insight unveiling how millions are made from trending cryptos, risk management trading mentality you need to imbibe to fortify yourself against getting burnt, a comprehensive guide on how to stay on top of the game and well detailed strategies on how to make a fortune with launchpads; these are some of the highlights of this illuminating book.

INTRODUCTION

The major preoccupation of crypto investors and traders is how to make informed moves and decisions that will ultimately lead to reaping the benefits from investing and trading in crypto currency. The book: 'The Cycle of Bitcoin Profit' is a comprehensive work to equip traders and investors in cryptocurrency with the critical knowledge, strategies and techniques to understand and decode market trends within the bitcoin ecosystem for maximum gains. The content is value loaded and includes basic principles such as market cycle, its longevity, bear and bull market and other foundational principles for winning big in the crypto turf game.

Cognizant of the fact that those who are successful in the crypto trading and investments are those equipped with timely critical information, techniques and knowledge, the book devotes substantial portion on critical themes; from basic knowledge of crypto currencies/blockchain (coins and tokens), Bitcoins, Ethereum, and Altcoins, staking coins, privacy coins, master nodes, etc., to rudiments of trading(Market news, products, team, community) to sufficiently equip traders and investors with the knowledge of when to buy and sell at a profit. The underlying principle is that it is best to sell when demand for a crypto currency is high and to buy when demand is low. It is demand or lack of it that determines why the price of a crypto currency can either swing up or down.

Trading cryptocurrency can be exciting and financially rewarding if set up properly and if you are conversant with the nuances, principles and techniques of cryptocurrency trading. If you have been off beat and wandering in the wilderness, the book will give you focus and direction. The book unfolds to you how to set up a crypto trading account, whether you want to carry out crypto to crypto exchange, exchange crypto for fiat or fiat money for cryptos.

As the book espouses, taking your trading or investment in cryptocurrency to the next level requires techniques and knowledge of platforms for digital currency and how to profit from them, how to gain from flipping IDOs, the importance of hot trending cryptos. One central theme that rings through in this book is how you can turn your efforts in the crypto trade into profit.

People constantly think of how to make enough money or income to take care of themselves, family and dependents. People within the crypto community are not immune to this and are constantly on the lookout of how to make the best profit. This book equips you with the knowledge and the necessary tools that you need to become a successful trader and investor.

What Is a Market Cycle?

Market cycles take place in all financial markets. But our preoccupation here is cryptocurrency. A crypto market cycle is simply the period between the peak and low of a market and in order to trade successfully, individual traders should watch these market moves or market cycles very closely. In this book, you will learn what to do when your cryptocurrency investments go on upward and downward swings. This knowledge is of vital, precisely because you will be needing it in the months and years ahead to nurture and make a success of your trading investments in cryptocurrency.

You should always bear in mind that whether you belong to the bull market (an investor who buys digital assets because they believe the market is going to rise) or the bear market (an investor who sells shares as he believes the market is going to turn negative), these market movements follow cycles.

For emphasis, bull and bear markets follow cycles which can last from 19 months to two years, with the longest cycle being the one we experienced between 2017 and 2020. And the market only began to enter into the bull market cycle towards the end of 2020. So, the end of 2020 marked the beginning of the bull market cycle.

Euphoria or despair is an indication of whether you are at the top or bottom of the cycle. Euphoria underscores the top of the bull market, a period when the market is at an all-time high while despair indicates that you are at the bottom of the bear market. Considering the above insight, the ideal move to make is to enter the market when there is despair and sell when there is euphoria. All you have to do is rinse and repeat to be fully soaked and engaged in the cycle.

How Long Do These Market Cycles Last?

The knowledge and answer to this question will help you know how you can perfectly time your entry and reap the benefits in the cryptocurrency trading space. Always have it at the back of your mind, the fact that bull markets are driven by the media and new investors. For instance, If the media space is awash with positive news about a particular kind of cryptocurrency, these positive, incisive analysis and news will ultimately drive new investors to invest heavily in that particular cryptocurrency. This huge impact on this cryptocurrency creates a positive impact on the industry as a whole. On the other hand, the bear market is driven by fear from both the media and the new investor. Typical of new investors, they buy from the top. Why? Because, the media with the information it unleashes and the frenzy associated with it, influences their behaviour. In effect, they buy a coin when the price is at an all-time high (ATH). Apart from the investors who fiercely believe in cryptocurrency, when the price plummets, a substantial number of these new investors will sell their cryptocurrency at a loss. Call it panic selling if you like, this panic selling spurns negative stories about an artificial cryptocurrency meltdown in the media. Many news outlets come up with apocalyptic predictions about the 'imminent collapse' of cryptocurrency, etc. The fact that cryptocurrency has ridden the waves of this negativity and emerged stronger demonstrates its resilience and forever staying power.

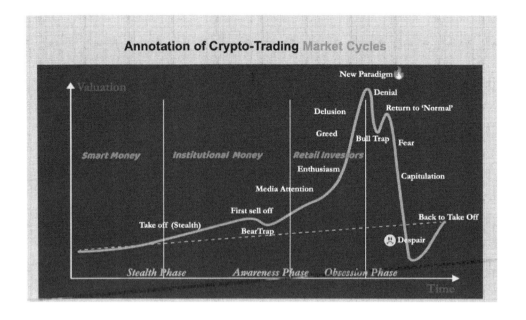

Fig. 1: A Typical Look and Feel of a Market Cycle

As shown in Fig.1 above, the crypto market cycle is shaped by time and valuation. As a smart investor, you should buy coins at the bottom, which in this case is the take-off or stealth phase, when there is despair. A period where nobody is talking about the market, a period of absolute quiet about the cryptocurrency space. This is where veterans (smart movers) start stacking up their portfolios.

After the negative media attention wears off, the coin(s) prices begin to surge but some people cannot believe what they are seeing, that this is for real and begin to sell off their positions. The behaviour by people who are bearish is called ' bear trap.' They sell off but the price only drops a bit then starts accelerating even further and exceeds the value of the first sell off.

The price of the coin continues to soar to the extent that it commands media attention, a period or phase that now ushers in institutional investors. This provokes a fundamental shift in the media as the once cynical media now begins to churn out positive news about this new wave, thus building enthusiasm. This development, naturally attracts the attention of the public, otherwise referred to as retail investors. They buy in towards the end, when a new paradigm, has been realized. This new enthusiasm is then fuelled by greed and delusion, the feel-good syndrome which has people thinking of achieving instant wealth. They begin to fantasize about becoming instant millionaires and billionaires. They invest under this euphoria. And while they are still at it, the price goes down, recording their first denial. It hits them hard at first. They are not yet ready to face reality. But gradually and surely, a bull trap creeps in. In this period, investors who are bullish hold onto their cryptocurrency and refuse to sell. They hold this unshakable belief that the prices are going to go back up. Things then appear to be normal but only for a while, but as resistance builds in, fear creeps in with the realization that they may not be right after all. Which further triggers a massive sell off capitulating down to nearly its previous take off price. At this point, the fall in the price of the coin provokes a backlash against cryptocurrency, bringing the entire market into despair.

Now, no person is immune to this trend, not even the veterans. So, from the very top, down to the bottom, there is a massive sell off which leads to the return of a new take-off.

The scenarios I have painted best illustrates what a bull and bear market cycle look like. Although some people think that the bull market lasts longer than the bear market, in practice, both last almost the same amount of time, between 19-24 months.

HISTORICAL ANALYSIS OF BULL AND BEAR MARKETS

In the beginning, Bitcoin had a price of zero when it was launched in 2009. On July 17, 2010, its price pimped to $.09. Bitcoin's price rose again on April 13, 2011, from $1 to a peak of $29.60 by June 7, 2012, a massive gain of 2,960% within three months. A sharp retracement in cryptocurrency markets occurred, pushing the price of Bitcoin down to $2.05 by mid-November. The following year, its price surged from $4.85 on May 9 to $13.50 by August.

2012 proved to be an uneventful year completely controlled by the bears, but by 2013 the bulls returned, and the market witnessed strong gains in price. Bitcoin began trading at $13.28 and reached $230 in the month of April, and then quickly taking a nose dive, bringing its price down to $68.50 a couple of weeks into the month of July.

In early October, Bitcoin was trading at $123.00; by December, the bulls took over the market pushing the price to $1,237.55, which later fell to $687.02 just 3 days into the bull run. Bitcoin's prices slumped through 2014 and touched $315.21 at the start of 2015.

Prices slowly climbed through 2016 to over $900 by the end of the year. In 2017, Bitcoin's price hovered around $1,000 until it broke $2,000 in mid-May and then moon-pumped to $19,345.49 in December.

This new milestone attracted the attention of Mainstream investors, governments, economists, even scientists took notice.

Bitcoin's price moved sideways completely controlled by the bears for two years plus, with small upward movement in price activity. For instance, there was a resurgence in price and trading volume in June 2019, with prices surpassing $10,000. This didn't hold for long, as the price fell to $6,635.84 by mid-December.

The global economy lockdown in 2020 propelled by the COVID-19 pandemic reignited the price activities of Bitcoin once again. The digital asset started the year at $6,965.72. The pandemic shutdown and subsequent government policy fed investors' fears about the global economy, didn't stop the bulls from pushing the Bitcoin price. By the end of year 2020, Bitcoin's price reached just under $29,000.

Bitcoin took less than a month in 2021 to smash its 2020 price record, surpassing $40,000 by January. By mid-April, Bitcoin prices reached new all-time high of over $60,000 as Coinbase, a cryptocurrency exchange, went public. Institutional interest further drove its price upward, and Bitcoin reached a peak of more than $63,000 in April.

By the summer of 2021, prices were down by 50%, hitting $29,795.55 at the lowest in July. The Bulls resurfaced again in September, scraping the price up to $52,693.32, but largely met with the bears price action dragging the price to $40,709.59 a couple of days later.

In November of 2021, Bitcoin again reached an all-time high, $67,549.14. only to be pulled down to $49,243.39 by the bears in early December amidst the emergence of a new variant of COVID-19, Omicron.

As a matter of emphasis, Bitcoin is still in its early stage and it would be premature to second guess the shape of things to come. But one thing is certain: Cryptocurrency and Bitcoin follow cycles. If the upswing is astronomically high with a dizzying spate, then it will ultimately lead to a dramatic fall. But if you time your entry perfectly, you could reap bountifully from the wave of this roller coaster ride. Now, let me sound a note of warning, **IT IS VERY IMPORTANT TO ALWAYS LOOK OUT FOR THE EUPHORIA STAGE WHEN EVERYONE IS JUMPING ON THE CRYPTOCURRENCY BANDWAGON. THAT IS THE TIME FOR YOU TO SELL.** Make sure that you don't miss it.

CHAPTER 1

SIMPLE GUIDE TO CRYPTOCURRENCY & BITCOIN

What is Cryptocurrency?

Cryptocurrency has been defined as a digital currency in which transactions are verified and records maintained by a decentralized system using cryptography, rather than by a centralized authority. Sounds vague? Let me try to break it down. Cryptocurrency is not physical currency; it is not like paper money or coins. It is a digital currency and not a tangible thing you can hold, store and go to a shop with to give to a salesman in exchange for goods and services. It is digital and is stored online in a blockchain.

What is a Blockchain?

A Blockchain, However, can be defined as a system in which a record of transactions made in Bitcoin or another Cryptocurrency are maintained across several computers that are linked in a peer to peer network. In effect, Blockchain is a public ledger of all transactions. So, the amount of Cryptocurrency you have as a result of your investment is stored on the Blockchain of that cryptocurrency. As I had stated earlier, the records are held in a decentralized system devoid of government or bank control. One of the marked differences between it and fiat (paper money) is that, it is not subject to or impacted by everything that impacts fiat (paper money) such as recession, Inflation, etc.

Cryptocurrency was invented in 2008 but the digital came into operation in 2009 when its implementation was released as an open-source technology. It was launched following the 2008 global financial crisis and the determination of people to take control of their money themselves, without relying on governments, banks and other financial institutions. It is a method of payment that is not impacted by centralized entities.

Bitcoin is the first known cryptocurrency. It is the most valuable and commonly held cryptocurrency with the rise in its value and popularity holding steady.

In 2008, the concept of Bitcoin was published in a white paper by an anonymous author that goes under the pseudonym *Satoshi Nakamoto*. The white paper outlined how Bitcoin would work. Today, Bitcoin has evolved and is the most popular flagship currency of all cryptocurrencies.

Apart from bitcoin, you have other types of cryptocurrencies. These include Ethereum, BNB, Dogecoin, Cardano, Litecoin, Solana e.t.c.

How To Get and Own Cryptocurrency

There are four main ways to get and own Cryptocurrency

1. Purchase on an Exchange

Buying on an Exchange is the major way people buy and own their cryptocurrency. An exchange is the market place where all the cryptocurrencies are, you can buy and sell; all you have to do if you are interested is to buy on an exchange.

2.Mining

Bitcoin mining is a process in which you deploy high powered computers that have the capability of solving complex mathematical problems. This is the process of creating new Bitcoin by solving a computational puzzle. When you mine any, it becomes yours. It has become a very sophisticated process necessary to maintain the ledger of transactions upon which Bitcoin is based. Mining is only possible if you have computer power, it is mostly carried out by mining factories.

3. Staking

You can own Cryptocurrency through this means. It is the process of delegating or locking up some amount of a certain Cryptocurrency for a period of time as a way to contribute to a Blockchain network to earn rewards.

Crypto staking can be likened to one depositing money in a bank. This is because the investor locks up his assets and the process, earns rewards or interest.

How do you do it?

First of all, you should download a wallet for the cryptocurrency, For example, Trust Wallet or Metamask and then buy BSCPAD token (a Binance Smart Chain Launchpad token) which is a coin related to an aspect of IDO – Initial Dex Offering on Binance Smart Chain. The next step is to put it in the staking wallet (Trust or MetaMask). By this move, you are helping run the Blockchain and as a reward for helping them run the blockchain, you are given free coins.

4. Rewards - Master node/platform actions

This is simply a reward delivered in crypto. Types of crypto rewards available for everyone include Active (staking, yield farming and investing) and Passive (Cashback, loyalty and gaming rewards, popularly referred to as "Play-to Earn'). In most cases you need a certain number of coins to be eligible to stake. This entitles you to a larger number of dividends. For example, if you are dealing in the Cryptocurrency called BSCPAD, you need a minimum of 1000 BSCPAD to be able to stake, which translates to about $2500.

What Is Bitcoin?

Going by its standard definition, Bitcoin is a digital currency which operates without the control of governments or banks. By its very nature, it relies on peer-to-peer software and cryptography. It is the flagship Cryptocurrency and sits at the very top of other cryptocurrencies. Bitcoin is actually a currency; you can pay for goods and services using Bitcoin. If someone for instance sells cars to you, you can pay with Bitcoin. It is a value currency. Every other coin is being measured in BITCOIN.

Bitcoin has gained wide acceptance globally since it came on stream in 2009. It is the currency most likely to be adopted by the mainstream. It is the flagship Cryptocurrency that has become the poster boy of cryptocurrency. Why does Bitcoin stand the greatest chance of being adopted by the mainstream? The reasons are many but the fact that it has been around for long and stood the test of time makes it all the more acceptable. Also, it has enjoyed an extraordinary journey, plus its value continues to increase.

If apple, google and a whole lot of other retailers want to incorporate Cryptocurrency into a method of payment, they will most likely settle for Bitcoin. What stands Bitcoin out is that it has had consistent growth. This consistency is in sharp contrast with more volatile Altcoins (alternative cryptocurrencies or Coins). One distinguishing feature of altcoins is that there are very volatile; they quickly go up and down. But, Bitcoin's record of stability is impressive. Yes, sometimes, it goes down but not for too long. When it comes back, it goes up again above where it was previously. Its growth has been consistent.

What is the reason for its exponential growth and consistency? First, it has a name and a solid reputation.

What Is Ethereum?

While bitcoin has been described as the king of cryptocurrency, Ethereum is seen as the queen of cryptocurrency. It is an open software platform which allows users to build a range of decentralized applications. It is different from bitcoin precisely because they don't have similar functions. There are probably thousands of Altcoins out there but Ethereum is the main Altcoin. It is a currency of value; you can use it to make payments.

Recently, a lot of platforms that have been created in the Cryptocurrency terrain are Ethereum based platform based on the Ethereum blockchain. Naturally, this development has conferred a lot of importance and value on Ethereum. Please bear in mind that Ethereum is like an operating system. For instance, if you want to build windows-based application, such as Microsoft word, it has to be compatible with the windows operating system. So, also Ethereum. It is simply an operating system which allows people to build platforms and apps. One other intrinsic quality of Ethereum is that it offers smart contracts. A contract is a written or spoken agreement especially one concerning employment, sales or tenancy. It is intended to be enforceable by law.

What Are Altcoins?

Altcoins are alternative cryptocurrencies launched after the success of Bitcoin. It is any other Cryptocurrency other than Bitcoin. One distinction to be made between Altcoins and Bitcoin is that there is high level of volatility trading Altcoins. What this means is that with Altcoins, things move up and down a lot faster and a lot more significantly. With it, it can go two times (2x) or twenty-five times (25x) in a day. How seismic the volatility or rise is, depends on how big the news of that particular Cryptocurrency is. If you invest in $SAND for $1 for instance, the same day, it can go from $2 to $6. This is driven by how significant the market news is.

Types Of Cryptocurrencies

As you are already aware, digital currency is gradually gaining acceptance all over the world as an alternative mode of payment to fiat currency. Cryptocurrencies are divided into coins and tokens. While tokens are built on an existing blockchain, coins operate on their own Blockchain and hold value as they are used as money for transactions.

Bitcoin, Ethereum and Altcoins as we have already learned are different types of cryptocurrencies. They have distinctive features that make them different and fall into different categories in terms of what they are.

Types Cryptos/Tokens/Assets

Staking Coins

This involves 'locking up' a portion of your Cryptocurrency for a period of time as a way of contributing to a Blockchain network. In exchange, those who stake will earn rewards either in form of additional coins or tokens. For instance, $BSCPAD

Privacy Coins

These are a class of cryptocurrencies that power private and anonymous Blockchain transactions by obscuring their origin and destination. As you are already aware, Cryptocurrency is meant to ensure privacy of transactions. Privacy Coins is a lot more confidential; it allows you to buy things privately and untraceable. It runs on a network that is untraceable. Monero, PIVX, Dash and Komodo are examples of some Privacy coins. So, if you are using privacy coins, it allows you to pay for your purchases with Cryptocurrency on a private network with the records not placed on the public ledger. Recently, the value of privacy coins has shot up, powered by a lot of people who do not want to pay taxes on their cryptocurrency.

Memecoins

A category of cryptocurrencies and tokens that are made based on a meme or was created as a joke. Typically, they are more of a community-driven phenomenon.

Their performance and growth are mostly linked to social media support, online community sentiments and hype created by influencers.

These memecoins are devoid of fundamentals and are highly volatile.

Examples: Dogecoin, Shiba Inu, Dogelon, Safemoon e.t.c

DeFi Coins/Tokens

These are digital assets that can be bought, sold, and traded using decentralized solutions called DApps. These tokens are created by the people for the people, without the government's upper-hand.

Examples:Uniswap ($UNI), Pancakeswap ($CAKE), Terra ($LUNA), Polygon ($MATIC)

Metaverse Coins/Tokens

These are a unit of virtual currency used to make digital transactions within the metaverse. Examples Sandbox ($SAND) Decentraland ($MANA), Bloktopia ($BLOK), Enjin ($ENJ), Metahero ($HERO)

Platforms

Crypto trading platforms are exchange platforms which allows the interchange of a digital currency for another. It also permits the exchange of a digital currency with fiat money. It is the second most valuable type of cryptocurrency. Platforms have utility and functionality. They allow you to get money for services you render. For instance, if you write blogs, you get paid for it. A platform is like a functional website and comes with a lot of value. It is imbued with revolutionary aesthetics in that it is trying to fundamentally impact and change services as we know it today.They are trying to revolutionize the way you make payments using fiat money by bringing already existing platforms to the Cryptocurrency world. Platforms are pivotal and have a lot of value. With platforms, you can be innovative because, when you add a bit of functionality, it makes it work better and allows you to get more money thus leading to the increase of the market value of Cryptocurrency in this field.

Builders

This is the most valuable cryptocurrency. This is external to bitcoin. Builders are the engine of Cryptocurrency since it is where most of the value is going to come from in cryptocurrencies. They are critically important. They enable companies to build their own software and platforms, to build a company using an operating system called builder cryptos. For example, Ethereum, Polkadot, Cardano, Solana, Polygon.

CHAPTER **2**

THE ESSENTIALS FOR BIG WINS: AN IMPORTANT INGREDIENT IN TRADING

The key to understanding this chapter is for you to know what drives the value of a coin. If you do, it will help you understand why coins are volatile and why it can have a massive spike without any indication. Crucial and at the heart of it, is demand. In economics, demand is an economic principle which refers to a consumer's desire to purchase goods and services and his willingness to pay a price for a specific good or service. Within the context of this chapter, let me quickly add that demand is the main reason why anything goes up and down significantly; if there is high demand for it, it will go up significantly and if the demand is less, it will decrease significantly. If anything is in hot demand, it causes a spike in the demand, it's as simple as that. For instance, when $ICP (Internet Computer) debuted, people were talking about it as if it is the next big thing, I basically put it in the same category as Ethereum. This sparked a huge interest and demand for it. The price shot up to $700+ from just $1 in a very short space of time. Lack of demand is what reduces the value of any cryptocurrency. So, demand is critical and central to price spikes.

Factors That Increase Demand for a Crypto Asset.

Market News

If you create a new innovation, a new wallet, new function(s) on your website that adds value; as a matter of fact, anything with positive impact, it can lead to a spike in demand. And a game changer constitutes market news that can trigger price hike. These developments can make that coin in demand for one day, one week. Under this circumstances, short term trading pounces by cashing in on the demand while it lasts. With a well-timed and well horned market news, a hitherto unknown coin can become an overnight sensation, driven as it were, from relative obscurity to prominence.

Cryptocurrency needs a strong marketing team composed of people who will consistently put the package on the consciousness of prospects with the right endorsements, commentaries and analysis. If a Cryptocurrency is value loaded and innovates but there is no way of letting people know about these values and innovations, there will be no demand. A proactive marketing team should be on hand to highlight and broadcast these innovations for it to have the desired impact which is to increase demand.

Products

People are with their thinking caps 24/7 and are consistently creating amazing products within the Cryptocurrency stratosphere. This is certainly the way to go, a sure way to increase demand. A good product essentially increases demand. If the product solves a real problem, it will certainly lead to a spike in demand.

Team

A good team is as good as a good product. People will always be swayed to invest in a particular Cryptocurrency if it has a star within its team. So, people naturally look out for any super star on the team. Take for instance, a mobile payment solution called XYZ comes on stream. If this mobile payment solution is designed to make payments in Cryptocurrency using your mobile. What would most likely drive demand for this product would be if they have a team member who has either worked for Stripe or PayPal, a major online payments solution company with global reputation. The person from Stripe or PayPal is their superstar. It's just normal for prospective investors to think of that, and feel if you have a superstar on your team, he could help you realize your vision a lot faster than if you just have a team of nondescript entrepreneurs with zero name recognition in the field of endeavour in which your project is tailored towards.

Community

This is very important. If you have a huge community, it is likely to spread the message. How can you for instance, get out your message with say twenty people in your community? how can twenty people impact a huge human population that runs into billions. But if you have a huge community of tens of thousands, and probably millions of people, then you can effectively get out your message. Their activities will basically help drive up the market. If you get into a Cryptocurrency community and you see and hear a huge number of people campaigning for a product, this is likely to increase demand for the product, and eventually spiking the price of product.

Trading Set Up Essentials

Trading in cryptocurrencies promises to be an exciting and financially rewarding experience if you set up properly. As a Cryptocurrency trader, you are involved in speculating on Cryptocurrency price movements through either a CFD (Contract for Difference) trading account or buying and selling the underlying coins via an exchange. To set up crypto trading, you require three things: Wallet, Exchange and Technical Analysis (TA) platform.

Wallet

A basic wallet that has a fiat gateway. What this means in simple terms is that with this basic wallet, you can buy Cryptocurrency with fiat money such as Pounds, Dollars, Yen, Euros, Naira, Rupees, etc. You can set up this wallet using Coinbase, Trust, Metamask. It actually depends on your country of origin. There are countries that can easily use Coinbase while in other countries it is practically impossible to use it. Where Coinbase cannot be used, Trust or metamask etc are good alternatives.

Leveraging the advantages of the wallet, you can send, store and receive cryptocurrency. From your wallet, you can send it to the exchange where you can if you want to, buy other ALTCOINS and cryptocurrency. You can also store it in there. One good thing about the wallet is that it is safe. If you want to receive some Bitcoin, you can do that with a basic wallet. There is no need to fear because it is secure. By its makeup, wallets are usually secure. One of the reasons for using a wallet is to protect yourself from being hacked. When you have done your trading, you should send it back to your wallet for security. It stays safe there until such a time you need to trade again.

Exchange

The second thing you need to get your crypto trading going is an Exchange. Once you have turned your fiat money into bitcoin or a tradeable stable coin, you need a market place to buy the ALTCOINS. This is the exchange, where you buy and sell. There are many exchanges from where you can buy your Cryptocurrency but the ones in hot demand include Binance, Kucoin, Bittrex, Bitfinex. These exchanges have a large index of cryptocurrencies. There are a lot of other exchanges out there but these ones do not have a negative reputation and are actually trusted to make your trading experience as seamless as possible.

Technical Analysis - Coinigy

It is in your best interest to use Coinigy for your technical analysis. If you are involved in trading on the short term, you should have your eyes on price movements as it unfolds. You may be trading for weeks or even hours. If you are trading for hours, then you should use Coinigy to find out the price movements. This will help you find out if the movements are bullish or bearish and assist you make the necessary investment decision in your best interest.

How To Buy and Sell Digital Currency

Buying and selling digital cryptocurrencies involves using one cryptocurrency such as Bitcoin, Tether (USDT), BUSD (Binance dollar equivalent) to exchange it for another Cryptocurrency such as Tatcoin on a buy and sell basis. Essentially, what this means is that as a crypto trader, you will be looking for a cryptocurrency pair that enables you to carry out a crypto-to-crypto exchange or exchange crypto for fiat or fiat currency for cryptos.

To perform this task, that is, to become a crypto trader, you need a wallet that has a fiat gateway. This enables you to use your own currency, be it Yen, Euro, Naira, Dollar, Pound, to buy bitcoin or USDT. The wallets with a fiat gateway are few indeed. All you have to do is to find out the one that is suitable and working in your country and use it.

Buy & Sell Crypto in Minutes: Binance Exchange as A Case in Point

Binance as you know is the largest Cryptocurrency exchange in the world in terms of daily trading volume of cryptocurrencies. In 2017, it was created as a utility token for discounted trading fees but its uses have expanded to numerous applications. These include payments for transaction fees on the Binance chain, travel bookings, entertainment, online services and financial services.

Binance used to be a crypto only exchange but has since become a fiat on ramp. The United States has a different Binance from the rest of the world. In the United States, you have Binance.us and for the rest of the world, there is Binance.com. If you want to buy crypto and have signed up to Binance, you can now buy with a credit card, debit card or with your bank account. Using Binance has obvious advantages but the advantages of using Binance over Coinbase are twofold. First, the fees payable for the service is slightly less than on Coinbase. This means that you will probably pay more crypto for your fiat money. The second advantage is that Binance has more Altcoins available for you to buy with your fiat currency. There are also a number of currencies available on Binance that may not be available on Coinbase. On Binance, there are way more options for fiat currency to crypto. If you are ready, all you have to do is to buy it directly with your fiat currency. What this means is that you are able to trade it directly on Binance. If you want a Cryptocurrency that is not on Coinbase, all you have to do is to send, for instance, your Bitcoin, Ethereum or Litecoin over to Binance, thus paving the way for you to trade it for another cryptocurrency. After purchasing the Cryptocurrency of your choice from Coinbase, you can then trade it easily with other Altcoins on Binance.

Interestingly, this transaction takes place in one place. Trading on Binance saves you the trouble of trading in two or more places with the potential risks of you losing your funds in the process. Transfer, ordinarily, shouldn't be a problem but some people who are starting out newly are prone to making mistakes. Some of them are actually confused about such basic tasks as public addresses and how to send cryptocurrency. This panic mode can make them miss out on a lot of cryptocurrencies on offer.

If for example, you can't buy a particular Cryptocurrency you want with your fiat currency in the fiat gateway of Binance, all you have to do to buy that particular currency, is to first buy USDT or Bitcoin and then trade it for other Cryptocurrencies on Binance.

CHAPTER 3

THE IMPORTANCE OF CURRENT NARRATIVE AND TRENDING CRYPTOCURRENCIES

If you want to make money in cryptocurrency, you need to understand what crypto players are currently interested in and where the big money is going. Understanding narratives and conversations is a major key to understanding the technology people are currently interested in and the flow of big money. In basic terms, narratives and conversations involve stories in Cryptocurrency indicating the role of emerging technologies in making it more exciting and therefore the best place to invest your money for multiple gains.

With the overall cryptocurrency projects story in mind, let us look into the previous, current and prospective narratives and conversations. What has happened before, during and after every conversation.

Bitcoin

The first narratives surround Bitcoin, the most remarkable Cryptocurrency in history. As Bitcoin has grown, its community has supported various narratives right from its early stages of invention. Bitcoin became a narrative at inception because of what it offered and meant to the world at the point of its coming on stream. It came through as a digital form of cash, completely uncontrolled by government and centralized entities. It soon came into prominence and became the unarguable leader of the Cryptocurrency industry. As a result of cryptocurrency, you are in control of your money and not subjected to interest rates, inflation, etc. Bitcoin is without a doubt the poster boy of this Crypto revolution. And it has weathered all odds to keep soaring and waxing strong. Its ability to redefine itself in the minds of its users is its strongest footstool.

Ethereum

This brought into Cryptocurrency so many beneficial features. It is more about technology and at present the second most traded and most valuable cryptocurrency. As the world's programmable blockchain, it built on Bitcoin's innovation with some big differences. Ethereum's configuration and the services it renders, enables businesses to grow out cryptocurrency, gain funds through the Ethereum Blockchain and ICO process. Ethereum also offers technology for people to develop businesses, to develop blockchains thereby enabling business activities.

Between 2015 and 2019, it made waves around the world and since then it has led to the birth of ICOs boom which was at its height in 2017/2018 and the DeFi boom in 2020.

It has enabled new industries to come on stream. Thus, electric and car companies, banking companies and website companies, gambling companies flourished as a result. So, Ethereum enabled these companies that had operated following the norm, come into Cryptocurrency with the aid of Blockchain technology. This gave birth to utility tokens that could be used on certain platforms.

Scaling is also another ripple effect of the entry of Ethereum into the crypto market. As a result, companies started expanding into the Blockchain ecosystem.

This ICO boom led to the creation of a lot of new tokens powered by new technologies. Ethereum and ICOs were part of the big narratives.

The year 2020 will be remembered as the year that gave birth to decentralization in technology. It gave birth to decentralized exchanges (DEX).

DeFi & NFTs

 NFTs stands for Non-Fungible Tokens. An asset is considered fungible when its units are interchangeable with one another. This means that they are indistinguishable. In other words, an asset class is fungible when each unit of the asset has the same validity and market value. In general, most cryptocurrencies are considered fungible assets. On the other hand, non - fungible means that it is different; it is unique and can't be replaced with something else. A non -fungible token (NFT) is a unique identifier that can cryptographically assign and prove ownership of digital goods. Examples of non -fungible token include a one-of-a-kind trading cart, a digital collectible, domain name, a ticket that gives you access to an event or a coupon, an in-game item, unique digital art work, etc. Essentially, Non-fungible tokens are digital collectibles.

DeFi was and remains the game changer, it made a big difference in decentralization.

It dramatically changed everything; it enables people to be their own bank. With decentralization imbedded in Bitcoin, it was about owning and having custody of your money. Whereas in the traditional world, they offer a whole gamut of services such as banking services, loans, high interest rates, savings and current accounts, etc. They tend to favour the wealthy with more services.

DeFi enables people to do the same without any barriers to entry. In the traditional banking world, you may not be able to participate in some businesses if your net worth does not meet the minimum requirement. With Defi, there are no barriers to entry as long as you are of age to be able to deal with cryptocurrency, you are allowed to participate.

DeFi enables people to be their own bank and receive greater profit than is obtainable in the traditional world. In some banks you earn annual interest of 0.6% on your savings.

In cryptocurrency, the starting point for your earned interest is from 10%. The possibilities are indeed huge and tantalizing. There are some high yield farms in which, if you stake your cryptocurrency, you will have a high yield. For instance, if you stake $20,000 and the yield is 500%, you can make as much as $100,000. The yield in Cryptocurrency is super bumper. The good news is that NFTs are in the process of coming out with its digital collectibles Some big celebrities have already come up with their own NFTs and selling their own collectibles using cryptocurrencies and NFT market places such as OpenSea.

The Sub narratives include PolkaDot cryptocurrency. As you already know, DeFi is mainly hosted on Ethereum Blockchain leading to high gas fees. When people want to trade, interact for lending and borrowing, the gas fees/ transaction fee is indeed high for Ethereum. This has prompted people to start using Binance Smart Chain where the fees are very low and at times non- existent. The other sub narrative is the speed and gas fees. This has led to interest in other blockchains such as Harmony, Avalanche, Solana etc. This behaviour is driven by the constant quest to find the best exchanges similar to Uniswap which is an Ethereum's decentralized exchange.

People are constantly searching for the next Uniswap from other ecosystems. They are searching for what is popular now and what is likely to be popular in the near future.

STOs (Security Token Offerings).

These are tokens designed to either give you an appreciation of value and financial benefits. On the other hand, utility tokens are not designed to deliver financial benefits. Rather, they are designed to have utility on the platform they serve but they go up in value because of demand. STOs on the other hand are designed to give you value. With it, you are able to tokenize various appreciative assets such as real estate, exotic cars, etc. With STOs, you can own a fraction of an exotic car, property, etc.

In concluding this chapter, bear in mind that you have about 8000+ cryptocurrencies for you to choose from, invest, trade and do business. But you should look out for the ones that are likely to have multiple gains potential, the ones that are trending and popular. This is where the money is going now. Go for them.

MetaVerse

Everyone's talking about the metaverse.

Why? And what the heck does "metaverse" mean, anyway?

The word doesn't have a perfect definition at this point; but that's OK: the metaverse is a process of becoming, not just being.

When I need to give a concise explanation, I say this:

The metaverse is the internet evolving into a creative space for anyone who wants to craft experiences.

The keywords are experiences, space and creative.

Metaverse is a word that conjures different meanings to people: to some, it's an immersive virtual-reality experience within a persistent landscape; to others, a specific technology stack; to some, it is a vision of future society.

The metaverse is the collective set of online, connected experiences that one can have. The common theme is that the "player" is connected to an online framework that permits live content changes, live social connection or live monetization.

The keyword is "live." The metaverse is a living multiverse of worlds.

The other "multi" is that the creation of games and virtual worlds has become multi-disciplinary, requiring knowledge of game design, game theory, behavioural economics, analytics, databases, music, AI, GPUs, graphics, branding, performance, user experience design, storytelling, software engineering and a hundred other talents.

Welcome to the metaverse: weirder, different and even more amazing than we originally imagined.

Decentralized Social Media

Decentralized social networks operate on independently run servers, rather than on a centralized server owned by a business. Mastodon is one example of a decentralized social network. It is based on open-source software and functions a lot like Twitter. Another example is Steem, which runs on a social blockchain. Blockchain technology allows data entries to be stored in servers anywhere in the world. It fosters transparency as the data can be viewed in near real time by anyone on a network.

Decentralized social networks give users more control and autonomy. An individual can set up their social network and determine how it operates and what users can say. Instead of having content monitored by a corporation, the founder of a federated social network can establish the terms of acceptable behaviour for the site.

CHAPTER 4

KEEP IT SIMPLE, STUPID; BUY LOW, SELL HIGH STRATEGIES

Essentially, there are a lot of ways to making money online with cryptocurrency. These would include; leverage on Bitcoin affiliate programmes, become active in the crypto industry, be an active trader, mine Bitcoin, carry out Cryptocurrency micro tasks, etc.

In this instance, we are dealing with how you can make a lot of money trading cryptocurrencies. For you to make a profit off this endeavour, you need to acquire trading strategies which you can apply and consistently make small gains and of course, huge gains. If you must maximize profits, while minimizing risks, it should be imperative for one to keep it simple, buy low and sell high.

Strategy #1: Capitalize on Demand, Supply for Profit

Anticipate Demand and Make Money from Trending Cryptos.

Opportunities exist for making money from trending types of cryptocurrencies. Essentially leaving you with an assignment of paying attention to common Cryptocurrency that have actually spiked and then putting extra research work to look out for cheaper alternatives.

There would normally come in groups and usually propelled by a given technological conversation or narrative, as I have earlier stated. Let us use staking coins as an example. If one staking coin is meant to be, people will rush looking for the next one. If you however get a cheaper alternative, you should anticipate a spike. If for instance you are looking for proof of stake coins and proof of stake wallet (POSW), don't chase the high of POSW. You should look for the one that has not popped yet but is the replica of POSW. It is likely to pop but if it doesn't pop, you have lost nothing but if it does, you will make a huge profit. This is exactly how you can make big money from trending cryptocurrencies. Your ability to anticipate a high is critical and imperative to your trading success.

Find Early Gainers and Profit from Them

Fig.2: An Extract from CoinMarketCap.com

Another way of making heavy profit from cryptocurrencies that are in demand now is by going into trending cryptocurrencies. If for instance you want to invest in YouTube videos, you should invest in the ones that are trending, the ones that people are flocking to watch right now. The steady flow of people rushing to watch that particular video has a snow ball effect.

It is important to go to Coinmarketcap and study closely, the biggest gainers and losers as shown in the illustration above. In Fig. 2 above, you will notice the circle to the left in the charts has four sets of information on the timeframe, viz; *1h, 24h, 7d and 30d*. In this instance, we are looking at a short- term trader action. And the best move here is to strike while the iron is red hot.

Essentially, what you have to do at this point is to go to the one-hour chart to see what is going on. While carrying out technical analysis of the performance of the cryptocurrencies, look closely at the biggest gainers. By paying sufficient attention on the gainers, you will learn about what is currently trending and what you can make money from. You should also note that sometimes, what ends up being the biggest gainer ends being the biggest loser, and this is so, because, it ends being pumped to such an extent that when it comes down, it becomes one of the biggest losers on the market.

There is no doubt that you can make big money if you perfectly time your moves but make sure you have your stoploss and/or good profit points in place. However, if your moves are driven by sheer greed, and you decide to stay on the trade longer than you should without a stoploss, you will record a huge loss, when that particular coin becomes the biggest loser on the market.

Furthermore, you should also pay close attention to the trading volume, analysing its highs and lows within the last twenty-four hours. Ideally, you should look out for projects that have six figures, which is an indication that it is receiving a lot of interest. If on the other hand it has low volume, what this means is that the coin supply is so low that a small increase of say $20,000 volume can lead to huge pump.

Above all, pay attention to projects that people are interested in. Finally, always look for the ones that have at least six figures or more but no less. If it is below six figures, it could be an indication that it has less demand.

Strategy #2: For Consistent Gains, Pay Attention, Plus Take Advantage of Every Gossip in The Crypto Space

Below are some simple but powerful pointers to achieving consistent gains.

Buy the Rumour, Sell the News.

If you effectively apply this trading tip, you can be sure of achieving best gains and consistently. Even if a Cryptocurrency or people from the community announce that something is going to come up; even if this information is announced in an offhanded manner, with specific information on date and time, don't be in a hurry to dismiss it. This announcement is the rumour, buy it. Note, also, that the actual date for the launch, be it of a wallet or rebranding for instance is the news. In effect, you are buying the announcement up to the news and what you should do is sell on/before the news comes out.

Depending on the impact of the news, you can make gains of between 20%-50% If for instance, a Cryptocurrency is being listed on one of the major exchanges, that in itself is a significant news with a huge impact. If it is just a new wallet, it makes a bit of impact and only affects those who are holders of that cryptocurrency. It is good news because it allows those account holders to keep their funds secure. A new wallet will not have a huge impact because it is on the lower end of significance but something that is a game changer, something that changes the nature of that Cryptocurrency such as rebranding or being listed on a major exchange is high impact. So, the number of gains you make depends on the level of impact and how long it holds.

Time Scale of Reaping Benefits

The time scale of when you can benefit from the news can be instant or it can take up to two weeks. Let's look at an example of instant profit. In November of 2021, a Cryptocurrency called Bosson Protocol, with a time period of 3 weeks, hinted they had something incoming for their community. The information wasn't clear. Normally when this happens, people begin to speculate which then leads to rumours. So, the hint was suddenly with the rumour of a huge partnership announcement.

Immediately the prices of Bosson Protocol pumped up to 2.5x from where it was at $1 to over $3.25.

As much as no one knew what to expect, or whatever it was, that was to be announced, people still went ahead to buy the rumour and some were smart enough to sell the news days ahead of the announcement day.

The second example is from Cryptocurrency called Power Ledger. In 2016, without prior information, they just announced that they are now listed on Bittrex, at that time, Bittrex was arguably the most popular western exchange. Immediately this announcement was made, the prices of Power Ledger pumped from $0.17 to $0.29 cents which is a huge leap.

It was certainly a significant news to be listed on a major exchange. Before being listed on Bittrex, Power Ledger which was relatively new at the time, was only listed on minor exchanges and was not the real deal. But its listing on Bittrex gave it a significant turnaround and enhanced its visibility. People instantly bought the rumour and sold the news. This news was instant. There was no time period to announce that its listing on Bittrex; Power Ledger just announced that it was already listed on Bittrex. Essentially, it was news and rumours at the same time and because it was straight news, people bought in. There was no indeterminable time by which it will start to tank. It started tanking when it was close to 30 cents. It tanked down to 25 cents but even at that, it was still a huge gain.

As I have emphasized here and based on the two examples, it can happen instantly or it can take two weeks of constant price rise. It can also drop the day or couple days before the news. The price can also rise on the rumour and dump way before the news.

The Actual News is the Dump

The actual news is typically the dump. What I am saying here is that no matter how significant the announcement, the actual news normally results in a dump. What happened to the price $DOGE off of Doge Father's (Elon Musk) SNL - Saturday Night Live appearance in 2021, a day the entire crypto space waited for the Tesla Boss to make a huge announcement that didn't happen, is a perfect example of speculation, rumours, price pump and an eventual dump.

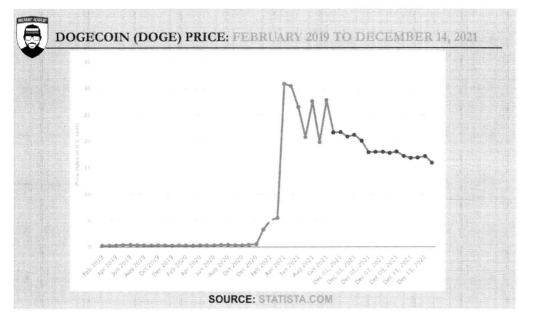

SOURCE: STATISTA.COM

Fig. 3: The $DODGE rise and fall of 2021

For some months, Prior to the SNL event, $DOGE was one of the fastest growing cryptocurrencies.

Specifically, and as illustrated in the chart above, between February of 2019 and October of 2020, $DOGE was in total obscurity but all of a sudden, it became one of the most sought-after cryptocurrencies. The price was not always at the level of $0.30, at a point, it nearly went up to$0.75 before it plummeted and is yet to recover.

Another example is NEO a Chinese based currency which was seen by some people as the Chinese equivalent to Ethereum. Although people liked it, its market focus was on eastern and north-western audience where a lot of people were pumping money.

Suddenly, people started hearing about NEO and at closer scrutiny,bh found out that it shared a lot of similarities with Ethereum. They started buying it but, in the run up to the announcement that there was a rebranding about to happen in 2016, the price went from obscurity, from being worth about 18cents to nearly $11 before it dumped on the news. It went from $11 down to $6. At a time, people praised the NEO branding as excellent, it was dumped heavily and the price went further down to $4. This is a textbook example that no matter how great a Cryptocurrency is, it gets dumped on the news because there is an opportunity to make a lot of money in the short term.

The pattern is instructive; it got spiked, dumped, spiked and got dumped again. Have it at the back of your mind always that people trade on the news. So, the number one trading tip is to buy the rumour. When something is coming up from a Cryptocurrency, buy as soon as you hear about it long before the actual date of the news. Buy the rumour and right before its starts declining which could be on the day of the actual news, get rid of it. You would have made your profit. Some people may be driven by greed to think that it can get dumped a little bit and spike again towards the day of the news. While this may be true, sometimes it never recovers. However, taking a guaranteed profit is better than waiting for a speculative one.

Strategy #3: A Market Crash Is a Perfect Multiple Gains Opportunity

Primarily, Investors buy assets (stocks/shares/coins) at a certain price, with the hope of selling those assets to realize capital gains. However, when the market crashes, it results in a sudden and dramatic decline in prices, which results in a significant loss on 'paper wealth. Sounds familiar right? Let's keep going.

Market Crashes in general are driven by underlying economic factors and/or panic selling, due to fear, uncertainty and doubt (FUD). However, it is one of the best windows or ways of making short term profits, if properly timed.

In cryptocurrency, the crash could be as a result of negative news about Cryptocurrency. Some influential voices in the world have ignorantly characterized Cryptocurrency as a fraud. One example is Warren Buffett negatively describing Bitcoin as "Worthless", "Delusion" "Rat poison" His statement which was characterized as demarcating sent jitters into the crypto market and prompted massive sell offs. The immediate effect is that everything went down and bounced up again. That was an opportunity for making money.

Market crashes are good in the sense that they are temporary. It bounces back when the fear disappears. That brief or intervening period is when you can increase your portfolio. So, instead of calling it a market crash, you should actually call it a Bitcoin fall. This could make a lot of people dump Bitcoin.

Essentially, market crashes are good for the Altcoins because it makes the prices to plummet and create an opportunity for you to make money off the bounce. As at the time when this work was in its preliminary stages, Ethereum was $2,900, BNB was $495, Solana was $169. So, they have all bounced back following the disappearance of fear. Market crashes are one of the best ways of making money because they always bounce back. Always look out for the high-quality ones and if you carry out your research well, get in at the right time, you will make great profits.

However, you need to be careful and avoid investing when the price is going to the bottom. Wait for it to bottom out. Constantly look at the market to see what is going on to make sure that you don't buy when the price is heading to rock bottom, so you could lose a lot of money if you mistime your moves. Then after your buy order is filled, you wait for the price to bounce and then you press 'Stop Loss'; if it bounces and goes down, you have not lost anything. If it goes up, you will make a profit. The success of the entire operation relies on attention and technical analysis.

Strategy #4: Community Profiting

A lot of people in the crypto world are involved in community profiting. What is involved here is using the community to find out or get a pulse of what is likely to pump. And this you achieve via the following channels highlighted below;

Watch YouTubers

One of the ways of spotting pumping Cryptocurrencies is to watch YouTubers. Whenever YouTube influencers talk about Cryptocurrency, people tend to pump it even if it's for a very short time.

Owned Groups

You can create your own group. This is what a lot of whales do full time. This however depends on how much the people within the group have to throw into a Cryptocurrency. If for instance, you pump in two hundred bitcoins into a coin fifteen times, this can actually provoke or accelerate a price rise especially if the coin has a low coin supply. The whales will get behind it to spike the price, make a huge profit and then get out. If you have smaller amounts of money that can be thrown at a Cryptocurrency, then you need at least a thousand, ten thousand or more people in the community to get behind a coin. They put whatever they have behind it, agree on a sell price point and then sell en masse once it hits the agreed price. This in a nutshell is how most groups play the Cryptocurrency trading game.

P&D Groups (Slack/Telegram)

You also have organized units called Pump and Dump groups. Typically, they are a community of people operating in a Slack, Telegram, or Discord channel or one of the channels you have on a mobile app. What happens is that they organize a Cryptocurrency to Pump and Dump. Usually, these groups will take a Cryptocurrency which is probably over sold or under the radar and pump it. A top gainer of the day in Binance for instance, may be a relatively unknown coin that was pumped in an organized way. In that case a group of people with high amount of tradeable money come together to pump a particular coin.

This will prompt speculative buyers to take notice of the fact that it is pumping; they will go into it and cause the price to skyrocket. This is an organized pump which will trigger the curiosity of people to find out what is happening. It is a typical operation of pump and dump communities.

Let's take for instance, the case of a coin called $SLP (Smooth Love Portion). For over 9 months $SLP was in total obscurity without an upward price movement but all of a sudden, there was a spike and everyone is talking about it. The price kept surging only to dump harder than it pumped, leaving the inexperience traders with a lot of bags. You can however, immune-protect yourself from being burnt by setting a 'Stop Loss'.

Price Manipulation

Basically, what is involved here is price manipulation, it is that simple. In this type of operation, the price is not going up, because there isn't any significant news but because of the activities of pump and dump organized groups. The price at times can go up on a completely dead project. For instance, ZClassic coin went up 10x in 2018. Although the developer stopped working on it, a group of people got behind it and manipulated the price. They bought in, encouraged a lot of speculative buyers and pumped the price up. This is pure price manipulation without any actual value. All that happened was that, the group put a lot of money into it, made it volatile with upward swing in price by pumping it from $7 to $35 and now it is worth just about $0.12. This is exactly how to profit using a community. Some of these communities charge you before you can be part of them. They don't take anybody; they admit people with a lot of disposable income.

Strategy #5: Swing Trade Profiting

Swing trading is a short-term investment strategy which people deploy to profit from swings in an asset's price. It can be profitable but it also has its drawbacks.

The focus in swing trading is on short term trends to achieve gains. Rather than attempt to get in and out of a trade in a day, or invest for the long term, a typical swing trade will take place over the course of more than one day and up to a few months.

Trading Coin Price Swings for Gain

It is a bit like buying the rumour, and selling the news. If for instance, there is a rumour that something is going to happen to a coin in two weeks; within those two weeks, there is going to be swings with the price going up and down. Towards the actual day, it really goes up and goes down on the day of the actual news. Now during those price swings in which the price goes up and down, you can essentially trade the same coin over and over. You can trade the price swings and make profit every time; if it goes up 4%, you trade it, it dumps, you make a profit on the rise. This is exactly how to do swing trading on the short term. It is more of a day-to-day kind of transactions. It is a very short- term strategy that enables you to make incremental gains.

Raise Holdings: Sell High & Buy Back Cheaper

On a long -term basis, people use swing trading to actually sell at a high and when it dumps, buy a lot of it back thereby increasing their positions. For instance, I have a hundred-thousand-dollar coin and it goes up to one dollar, that means that I have $100,000. If that amount is at all-time high, I can sell my large number of coins in that cryptocurrency. If it goes down to 85 cents, with my $100,000, I could buy a whole lot back so that when it goes up to a dollar again, I make more money.

That's how people trade on a long- term basis. If for instance you bought 30,000 worth $SAND and the price really spikes and you are thinking that you should have bought a hundred thousand worth of the $SAND. You can dump your coin, sell at a high thereby making a profit. With the profit you have made, you can buy back a lot more for less money when it dumps. This is how it works on a long- term basis.

Buying Oversold, Selling Overbought

Another way of doing swing trading is to buy when something is oversold and sell when it is Overbought. It is a lot easier to do. A coin is oversold when people have been selling it too much to the extent of dumping it to the bottom. You then buy the bottom, and when it goes back up, gets overbought, you can then sell, and then rinse and repeat.

Majority of traders apply this approach, what they simply do is use RSI research tool, which enable them see that a particular coin oversold. These traders then buy a lot of it and it then gets overbought, made even so by the entry of a lot of speculative buyers and long-term investors. It is essentially a long-term position because it can take days, weeks or even months to go from oversold to overbought.

A lot of traders in this bracket make their full-time income using this strategy. A lot of them are whales who have built up an impressive financial war chest off bitcoin. So many of these traders have been part of the Cryptocurrency revolution from the onset. What they do essentially is to use these bitcoins to deposit large amounts in a cryptocurrency. Whenever it makes a little spike, they make a huge profit out of that even if it is three to five per cent. Traders can actually make full time income from swing trading.

Strategy #6: Margin Trading

Essentially, margin trading is the use of capital borrowed from a broker to invest in something such as cryptocurrency. In recent years, it has become increasingly popular. One of the huge advantages of margin trading over regular trading is that it allows you to gain access to larger sums of capital and leverage your position.

It is popular in a lot of exchanges. People are involved in margin trading because they do not have enough money to invest in cryptocurrency to make huge gains. If for instance, they know that a coin is going to pump and naturally wants to put a lot of money behind it. They don't have the money, so they borrow from a broker to pour into the cryptocurrency and then be able to trade on the price swings.

So, if you know that a coin is going to pump but you don't have enough money to invest and make huge gains of 50% or even 2000%, what you need to do is that you borrow. But you must be sure of the pump. Be certain, that there is some market news, or there are pump and dump groups behind it. So, you need to be certain that the pump is going to happen to make it worthwhile. Otherwise, if you lose what you borrowed, you will become a debtor.

Margin trading tends to be available to margin buyers. If you are a small-time trader, you won't be accepted. People with a million net worth and beyond are those who are accepted and/or those who engage in margin trading. Your credibility must be such that, the brokers know that you are more likely to pay them back. It is available on Binance, Kucoin, Poloniex and other exchanges.

CHAPTER 5

TAKE YOUR TRADING TO THE NEXT LEVEL: MASTER THE EXTRA TECHNIQUES AND STRATEGIES APPLIED BY CRYPTO VETERANS

In this chapter, we will explore other opportunities that abound in venturing into ICOs, IEOs and IDOs, while scrutinizing the techniques and strategies crypto veterans have continually used to accumulate wealth for themselves.

Approach #1: Flipping ICOS

Initial Coin Offering (ICO) is simply a form of Cryptocurrency used by businesses to raise capital. Under this arrangement, investors receive unique Cryptocurrency tokens in exchange for their monetary investment in the business. In other words, Initial Coin Offering is a means of crowdfunding through the creation and sale of a digital token to fund the development of a project.

As you get deeper into the strategies for day trading, the steps you should take to make money in trading both day trading and short-term trading is ICO flipping.

Why Trade ICOs

This is the first time you can buy Cryptocurrency when the price is at its lowest. If you buy for instance when the price is at 2 or 3 cents, that gives a lot of room for the Cryptocurrency to grow to let's say fifteen, twenty cents and infinitum. That way, you can really make a lot of money with ICO - Cryptocurrency because of its flexibility and strong possibility for growth. This incentive is the reason a lot of people are involved in ICOs. However, there are factors which influence the performance of strong ICOs. These factors help traders make investment decisions. For instance, it would be a 'NO, NO' for an investor if an ICOs struggles to make its ICO target or hard cap target or even struggle to get enough buyers into it.

Approach #2: Flipping IDOs For Massive Gains; The Opportunities In 2021 And Beyond

As tokens, Initial Dex Offerings represent any type of asset hosted on a decentralized exchange (DEX). An IDO is when a project launches a token through a decentralized liquidity exchange. IDOs remain the best way to get involved in early-stage projects. And one sure way to get involved in IDOs is through various websites or better still launchpads platforms. A few examples of these platforms are polkastarter, BSCPAD, Seedify, GameFi, DAOmaker Paidnetwork, Adapad, MetaVPad, Astronaut etc.

Each of these platforms have their requirements for IDO participation, mostly categorized in a tier system. Which means, for an individual to be eligible to partake in an IDO, you will be needing a certain number of tokens, if you must define your category of tier. The tiered system is structured to create the different levels for IDO allocation and also to limit the number of persons that can participate in a given IDO exercise.

Unlike the ICO or IEO, all prospective participants must conduct a KYC exercise and also stake their tokens for a period of time and that again depends on the launchpad. For instance, for you to be able to participate in an IDO project on BSC LuanchPad, you will need to purchase a certain amount of BSCPad tokens, and then stake them for a minimum of 3 hours before the IDO opens. Anything other than this you can't participate.

If you can get into the bandwagon early enough, you will be able to flip it almost immediately. If you get involved at the IDO stage, you will get Cryptocurrency at a rock bottom price. Some of these project offerings have done well. Take for instance MetaVPad. If you got involved with it at IDO stage, you would have been able to get its tokens for 0.001cents. Today, MetaVpad token is worth $1.30.

If you get into a project with a lot of venture capitalists backing it, and strong community behind it, then you are practically on a home run. In order to gauge the level of public interest in a project, how big the community is and how they are talking about it, you can join telegram groups which affords you the opportunity of doing all these and much more. These interactions will give you an indication of how hot the particular Cryptocurrency is. If you are buying now, it certainly means that you are going to spend a little more now. For instance, BSCPAD (Binance smart chain IDO Launchpad) token costs about $2.40 and you need ten thousand (10,000) of them, which is about $24,000.

Different Launchpads differ in their requirements; you may in an instance need 10,000 BSCpad

There are two ways to get involved in IDOs. First, you can be involved in IDO stage which will require that you use the Launchpad. Secondly, you can get involved as soon as it is launched on pancakeswap or Uniswap. You need to be in a Telegram group to know when the announcement is made live and get into it quickly in order to harness the benefits of early participation.

Aproach #3: Flipping new Coins for Maximum Gains-How to Spot Hot ICOs, IEOs, and IDOs

If you want to invest in **ICOs, IEOs, and IDOs**, you should be guided by certain criteria which will help you determine and differentiate the poor-quality projects from the bright ones that command demand and can sell out very quickly. In arriving at this conclusion, you should ask questions such as:

Demand

Demand drives and at the same time differentiates the strong performing projects from the weak or worthless ones. If people are talking about it, even though it has just been launched, this phenomenon can only mean that the crypto is in demand.

A good example of an ICO which sold out is STRATIS. The demand for STRATIS was astronomical with every active player within the crypto world talking about it. This offering set Twitter on fire; also, the three main Cryptocurrency communities on Facebook were heavily talking about it. Upon launch, the effect was simply amazing with everybody wanting to get behind it. One of the reasons for this phenomenon is that it effectively marketed the various qualities that made it a valuable cryptocurrency. As a matter of logic and predictability, people quickly get behind a Cryptocurrency with a lot of demand. What this means is that they may be flooding the exchange to sell which may not necessarily sell. Here is the deal: while they may not actually sell, they will go on exchange to prove that they are actually tradeable and can actually sell if need be. As a result of the demand for it, people will naturally look out for the day that it debuts on the exchange. If this high demand holds through, what it means is that you will witness a peak selling season. So, demand is a huge factor when it comes to ICO flipping.

If you want to know the factors that are driving and stimulating the demand, all you have to do is to simply join Cryptocurrency groups to see and feel what people are hyping about. You can even throw questions to the group to find out what is being hyped and why it is being hyped. From answers to your questions, you can easily deduce or gauge what is more in demand.

The Project

The project itself has the capacity to drive and influence demand. Questions that could be asked is whether the project is a trending project.

SANDBOX is one of the major trading Cryptocurrency on METAVERSE platforms and a lot of people have made money investing, trading this Cryptocurrency. You need to also know that if a project coming out corresponds to recent trend or current Crypto conversation, this makes it more in demand and critically, improves its prospect for success. Presently, SANDBOX is in-demand Cryptocurrency, although it is not the best cryptocurrency.

Remember that a lot of time when you invest early in a cryptocurrency, you are usually rewarded with a bonus. Let's use BNB as an example. Today, it costs $600 to buy one $BNB. But if you had invested in the early stages, you could have gotten it at a cheaper cost. Meaning if you were among the first one million token buyers, you could have got it at less than 10 cents.

Community, Support and Hype

The size of the community groups (the cryptocurrencies Facebook page, Twitter page, their Telegram channel, etc.) are also of critical importance for you to know and appreciate better the market trends. If these communities have a lot of people, this will simply mean that their swelling membership will increase demand for the much talked about product. A lot of people talking about a product, lot of communities/people behind a particular product on offer can only translate into a lot of sellers.

If an ICO has a community, it then means that the price has a mechanism for stabilizing. It is in a way insulated from dramatic volatility because it draws huge support from its community. If the price goes up and then drops, the support line from the community will hold, thus preventing it from going down too badly. Hype in question here means that there are people who are excited about the ICO. The belief in it gives it value. The existing support base helps to protect the price of the crypto.

Available Supply & Price Per Token

The smaller the supply, the greater the volatility and the more the price will rise if volume is pumped into it. If for example you get in when the price of a coin is 5 cents, when it is on low supply and people pump in a lot of funds, the price could go up easily to 1$ because it is on low supply.

Being on low supply means that the volume that is pumped into it will affect the price volatility and drive the price way up. It can also make the price go down violently.

If the supply is relatively modest, say in nine figures or less, that's great, but if it is in ten figures and above, that is not good enough for short term flippers. The point to be made here is that, if you get into a crypto project at a low price per token, you can make huge profit right on the first day.

Superstar(s) Investors/Members/Advisors

As I had stated earlier, Superstar members on the Advisory board or Superstar Venture Capital Investors come with star quality which generates confidence in the ICO. Clearly, their presence on the project can make a huge difference. For Instance, Let's take a look at the newly launched metaverse project called BLOKTOPIA.

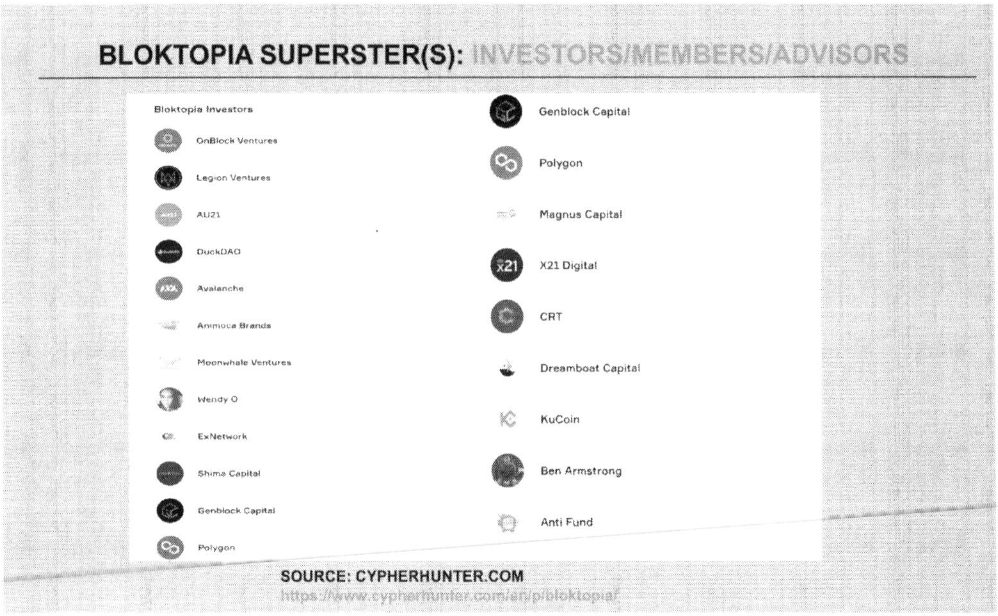

BLOKTOPIA SUPERSTER(S): INVESTORS/MEMBERS/ADVISORS

Bloktopia Investors

OnBlock Ventures

Legion Ventures

AU21

DuckDAO

Avalanche

Animoca Brands

Moonwhale Ventures

Wendy O

ExNetwork

Shima Capital

Genblock Capital

Polygon

Genblock Capital

Polygon

Magnus Capital

X21 Digital

CRT

Dreamboat Capital

KuCoin

Ben Armstrong

Anti Fund

SOURCE: CYPHERHUNTER.COM
https://www.cypherhunter.com/en/p/bloktopia/

Fig. 4: Bloktopia "Superster' Investors

Bloktopia is a Decentralised Metaverse designed to provide an unprecedented VR experience for the crypto community, bringing users together in an all-in-one immersive and engaging environment. The cryptocurrency project is a product of Polygon-Matic blockchain, a blockchain company that is currently worth $19 Billion. For a smart crypto trader, this is a no brainer.

As shown in the Fig. 4 above, veteran traders wouldn't look any further on discovering that BLOKTOPIA is not built by Polygon, but it is backed by numerous VCs and more so, KuCoin, a top Crypto exchange in crypto space.

Having the above superstars on a project is a huge leap to success. It is no surprise therefore that BLOKTOPIA presale sold out immediately it hit the crypto space.

Uniqueness

Another quality to look out for is uniqueness and the question to be asked is whether the Cryptocurrency stands out. A Cryptocurrency with first mover advantage is clearly desirable because what it means is that the price volatility could be much higher. People are not interested in investing in what has been done before. It doesn't just stand out. Its lack of newness dilutes the demand because there is already competition.

To a lot of people, Binance ($BNB) remains the best cryptocurrency investment ever; they created universal wallet. This was in addition to fiat exchange. It created a place where you could buy all Altcoins and swap one currency for another. At the beginning, there range of services were unique in that they were the only ones doing it. A lot of people invested heavily in it and reaped so much because the price went up thirty times

Vision

Your vision is important and will determine the success or failure of your endeavour. People often ask how they can become millionaires in six months or in a year. The answer is simple: *proffer a solution for a problem of a million people and charge them a dollar for it and you become an instant millionaire.* In order words, all you have to do is to find out a paying point that exists in the market.

One of the greatest challenges in the Cryptocurrency business is security, everyone wants a place to secure all their cryptos. Wallet is one place that you can secure your cryptos. Millions of people are involved in Cryptocurrency trading/investment and are concerned about the safety of their investment. They require a place to buy, store and a place to turn their fiat money into cryptocurrency. The truth about it all is that if there is no paying point, there is no demand. Producing anything that nobody wants is an exercise in futility. It is therefore of vital importance that you look for something that a lot of people want and are ready to go for it. If you are able to achieve it, then you have created a solution and therefore a good paying point. If it is on a scale that millions are affected by it, this will definitely drive up the price for it. This in a nutshell is the difference between a rubbish and an exceptional ICO/IEO/IDO Project.

6

FLIPPING NEW COINS (IDOS AND PRESALE) FOR 100X - 1000X GAINS THROUGH LAUNCHPADS

For a better understanding and appreciation of how to make profit by flipping new coins using Launchpads, it is necessary to understand fully what Launchpads and IDOs/Presale are in cryptocurrency. There are some crypto platforms that help investors discover early-stage crypto projects before they enter the mainstream. These crypto platforms are known as Launchpads.

Between 2017 and 2018, there was a process called Initial Coin Offering (ICOs) which essentially was where a project made it possible for retail investors and whale institutional investors to get involved in cryptocurrencies at rock bottom prices before they enter the exchanges where the demand pumps into the exchange and the price skyrockets. But these days, LaunchPads have taken over. You can use LaunchPads for either short- term flipping or for long term investment. There are many LaunchPads out there but, its use is dependent on what blockchains you want to buy the cryptocurrency. Ethereum, Binance Smart Chain and Polkadot are perceived to the best Blockchains. Among the newly established LaunchPads are Cardano and Polygon.

It is best for you to use LaunchPads If want to get involved in early-stage cryptocurrencies, from different blockchains.

What Are Launchpads?

This is where you buy cryptocurrency tokens at IDO price. It is important to note that you can only get them on specific Launchpads.

What is Tier in an IDO?

The Tier is a system that comes with options that enables you to get allocations which is the dollar amount that you can buy that cryptocurrency on the Launchpad. This, however is dependent on your chosen tier. If you are on the lowest option, the implication is that you will get lower allocation whereas if you go for the higher tiers or options, you will definitely get a higher allocation. This allows you make the best of multipliers or gains.

Requirements For Getting Involved in Launchpads

 It is important that you know the type of coin you need to purchase, in this regard, the Launchpad token which enables you to get into all IDOs that come on that Launchpad. You don't necessarily need to buy each IDO. The point to be made here is that once you purchase and stake the minimum required Launch token, you can get involved in all IDOs from that future point.

How To Use LaunchPads

The best way to shed more light on this process is to use a clear example to demonstrate how it works. It is important for you to understand and master it because it is the best opportunity to make money in cryptocurrency. A good example is the Polygon IDO, previously called Matic at a private sale stage. Those who participated got in at $0.002, which translated into a fifth of a cent. Today, polygon is at $2.20, a whooping 1000x from the Private sale rock bottom price. Basically, one thousand dollars with a 1000 x translates to one million dollars. This huge leap underscores the importance of getting into cryptocurrency at the earliest stage. If you enter at the very early stage, it allows you to get them at a rock-bottom bullet-proof price before the demand for that cryptocurrency kicks in. This is because, it is more lucrative to buy into this cryptocurrency at an early stage, than buying a cryptocurrency that is already in the top 100 which has already made money for early investors.

It certainly makes sense to be an early investor in a cryptocurrency with the potential of making it into the top 100 in the market.

In a nutshell, Launchpads are a great way of making big money either on short or long terms.

There are a number of Launchpads. These include:

Polkastarter: This concentrates on cryptocurrency which focuses on Polkadot ecosystem.

BSCPAD: This is the first decentralized IDO platform for the Binance smart chain network.

PAID: This concentrates on Binance, Ethereum and Polkadot.

POLYSTARTER: This is a fully decentralized project accelerator for Polygon.

These and many more LaunchPads offer great projects that you can get involved and make tons of money.

How To Participate in an IDO

The critical questions that need answers for you to understand how to get involved in IDO Launchpads are these: *what do you need to take part in IDO Launchpads? How can you directly buy cryptocurrencies at IDO price?* It is important that you understand that launchpads differ in the way that you access IDOs. For Polkastarter, you cannot get higher allocation than someone else but on BSCPad, there is a tier system. What this means is that the higher your tier, the better the allocations and that's for the guaranteed aspect of the tiered system. For example, on the lowest tier (Platinum, you are to purchase and stake ten thousand BSCPad tokens, and you have a very minor allocation. But if you are on the Diamond or Blue Diamond tier, you will get a much higher guaranteed allocation.

BSC Launchpad on average has delivered 78.5x on their IDOs, PAID Network has delivered 62.6x and Polkastarter has delivered 31.6x. A closer look at the BSCPad, its native token was launched on their own site. In effect, making it first ever IDO to get on their Launchpad. Whoever got in on this IDO, would have netted a gain of 330x. As a result of these, $1000 would have become $330,000.

Imperatively for project owners who are looking at launching their projects via IDO, it is worth knowing that as an early-stage project, it is vehemently advisable that you go to the most successful Launchpads to host your IDO price for your project. This will enable you have the best start you can. In the same vein, for retail investors, they definitely want to get involved in launchpads that deliver the best ROI (Return on Investment).

As you already know, with Initial Dex Offering (IDO), you are able to get an early-stage cryptocurrency at a low price before it gets listed on a Decentralized Exchange (DEX), for instance Pancakeswap, Uniswap etc. Once it is listed on a DEX, it tends to do well.

CHAPTER 7

BSCPAD MASTERY: GUARANTEED PATHWAY TO FLIPPING COINS FOR PROFIT

We are operating at the realm of possibilities where everything is possible. It is possible to get involved in IDOs directly. For the purpose of illustrating this reality, I am going to use BSCPad, the more popular and most utilized Launchpads in cryptocurrency. This Launchpad as you already know concentrates on early cryptocurrencies in the Binance smart chain block chain. Presently, there are a few block chains where cryptocurrencies are being released on. But, the two main ones are Ethereum (most cryptocurrencies come out on Uniswap) and Binance smart chain. The point to be stressed here is that when these cryptocurrencies launch from

Launchpad, they tend to go on pancakeswap. Before it goes on pancakeswap, you can be able to get it, hopefully, at a great discount with a Launchpad platform.

How to Use the BSCPad

The first thing to do if you want to use the BSCPad is to buy into a tier. BSCPad is the first decentralized IDO platform for the Binance smart chain network. There is no centralized control over the BSCPad, all you need to do is to follow the guidelines or steps which will enable you get involved. As shown in Fig. 5 below, it has a tiered system. So, if you must get an allocation, you have to buy into one of these tiers which come in categories. This is the minimum requirement.

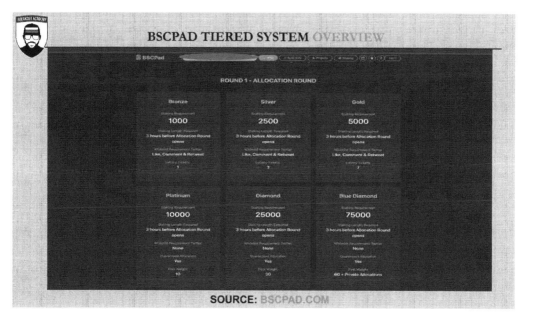

Fig. 5: BSCPAD Tiered System Highlight

You need a thousand BSCPad Tokens for the Bronze category, two thousand, five hundred BSCPad Tokens for the Silver category and five thousand BSCPad Tokens for Gold category. The higher tiers are from ten thousand BSCPad Tokens and above.

Essentially, with these tiers, all you have to do is to multiply one thousand or whatever number or category you want to invest in by the current price of BSCPAD token.

How The Tier System Works.

As you already know, there are fundamental differences between the tiers. For the bronze, silver and gold category, allocations are based on a lottery system, not guaranteed as opposed to the higher tiers. Prospective participants investors are required to like, comment and retweet about the project from BSCPad. With platinum, diamond, and blue diamond, you get a much higher pool weight. The Platinum category secures for you a guaranteed allocation with a pool weight of 10, Diamond has a pool weight of 30 and Blue Diamond has a pool weight of 60, plus, private allocation. The more pool weight you have, the larger the allocation. To arrive at the allocation that you want in terms of gains, you should weigh up or consider the cost versus the reward.

Mandatory Staking, KYC, BNB and BUSD Requirement

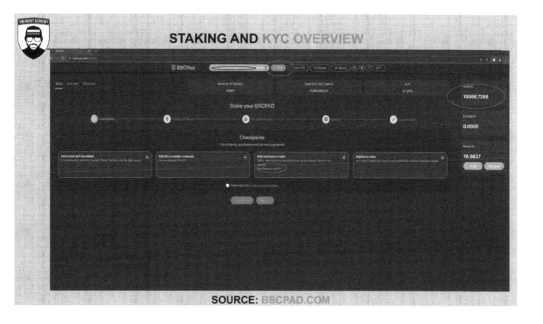

Fig. 6: BSCPAD Staking and KYC Interface

Once you have the required amount of BSCPad, you need to stake your tokens. If you staked your ten thousand BSCPAD tokens, you can get as much as 15% APY or 15% of rewards based on your allocation. In effect, you will get 15% of ten thousand back to you.

After staking your BSCPad, you need to connect Trustwallet or Metamask of which you must have deposited your BSCPad and then you will be eligible to stake.

The next step for you is to complete your KYC, by simply clicking the part on the dashboard marked KYC. The KYC button turns green when you have been verified. This process may take up to 72 hours. This process helps to establish the fact that you are not from one of the restricted jurisdictions barred from getting involved in IDOs.

One of the great things about BSCPad is that you tend to get new project every now and then. Therefore, there is always an opportunity to invest and make gains.

How To Practically Get Involved

The first step for you is to go into the actual page that allows you to invest. Essentially, these projects become available for you to invest in around 9:00am UTC time. To be able to invest in an IDO on BSCPad, you need BUSD which is the buying currency. Typically, there are two BNB or BUSD. The Binance coin is called BNB while BUSD is the Binance dollar. The Binance dollar is intended to always be relatively stable at $1. 500BUSD is projected to be 500US dollars. If you have been given 400BUSD allocation and it makes 100x, then the $400 would be $40,000. This is a huge allocation compared to what you get in some other Launchpads.

The general pool contains several details. There is the first come, first served pool which is a different pool and that opens after the main allocation round has closed. Once the timer goes down to zero. You must be quick, if you must grab extra allocations. It would normally open at 12:45 UTC, normally the same time every time. The general pool will also show you the cap, how much that is being targeted to be raised in this particular allocation round.

So, if you decide to participate after getting an allocation, that's if you are on guaranteed tier, then you need to approve first of all by clicking approve. You can invest any amount of your choice guided by the allocation that you have been given. For instance, if you have been given an allocation of $100, you can invest all of it or you can invest $50, or $70 as the case maybe. It is up to you but the point to be made is that you don't have to use your full allocation. But if you want to use your full allocation of $100, all you have to do is to click approve to approve it. This will take you to another screen where you have to pay a transaction fee for the approval to use your BUSD on this platform.

After you have done that, you will see 'approve success' which enables you to join the pool. Make sure that you have BNB for the gas fees which is relatively very low compared to fees of other cryptocurrencies. After the approval, with the swap rate at 1 BUSD equals the given amount of the

Crypto, let's say XYZ coin, it will give you the total amount based on the total allocation swap multiplied by the amount per BUSD. Once this pool finishes, then you will be able to withdraw that into your wallet claiming your tokens. Once it is in your wallet, then you can sell it once it becomes available on an exchange. In this instance, this will be on Pancakeswap. Once you have gone through this process, it is up to you to decide how you want to use your allocation.

Here you are faced with two choices, either to flip it in the short term or you want to hold onto it for a long term. The fact that cryptocurrencies are bullish the minute there are launched may influence you to sell. People tend to sell when the product achieves its first initial spike which makes it achieve its first high valuation. At this point, there are a lot of people in the market who just want to flip this for profit.

CHAPTER 8

BUILDING A FORTUNE WITH LAUNCHPADS

Launchpads have beneficial and transformative capacity if you know how to use them. You can actually amass a fortune if you use them in the most effective and efficient way. As we already know, Launchpads are really good for getting into IDOs for flipping. No matter which cryptocurrency you are getting in an IDO price which is a very low price with low market cap. In most occasions, it is difficult to actually see the price go down to IDO price. As a matter of fact, the price of most, if not all IDOs have never come back to the IDO price even when they lose a lot of value many weeks down the line. You can use IDOs as a way of flipping to increase your position into cryptocurrencies or projects you actually want to hold for long. In most cases, you will actually make at least 5x. This is almost guaranteed. If for instance, you had an allocation of $50, after the IDO launches, then you will get at least one thousand dollars. In many of these cases, you could get $50,000. What this means is that, if you like a Cryptocurrency that you have been planning to buy, you can sell that IDO for 2x -10x and take a bigger position in something you actually want to hold for a long term.

The second-best option is to plan for long-term investing when you see a project and you then prospect it to have potential. When you are deciding what Launchpad to get in and what Cryptocurrency you can take a long-term investment in conjunction with research on CYPHERHUNTER.COM. This way you can bullet-proof your funds by looking out for various IDOs that will serve your purpose. Like I mentioned earlier about Bloktopia. At a glance, you can see who has invested in $BLOK. The caliber of people who have invested in it will give you a good indication if it has a long-term potential or not. It will also inform you if they have got VCs who are likely to fund them for the long haul and deliver a lot of value in the end.

The presence of VCs on a project is certainly great news for long term investors like you and me. So, for cryptocurrency with a lot of backing, you may not be in a hurry to flip it for a quick profit. You could also sell it once it launches because hours into the launch, its performance is at its best. You can sell it near the top and after the first couple of hours or days of great performance when the price drops significantly, you can buy back and take an even bigger position.

These possibilities are available to you as a result of Launchpads.

Having looked closely at Bloktopia, I believe that they have decent investors and are therefore good for long term investment. On projects that have a lot of promise, it is better to have a bigger allocation so that you can make massive gains when you decide to cash in.

CHAPTER 9

RISK MANAGEMENT: ACTIVE STEPS AGAINST GETTING BURNT

People are deeply concerned about how they can trade/invest in cryptocurrency without getting burnt. We have been inundated with hefty guides about how to protect your bitcoins against theft and hacks. We have equally been taught how we can effectively trade on cryptocurrency and make those astronomical gains that people can only dream of. We have been told to make a cryptocurrency brokerage account, fund our account, pick the cryptocurrency to invest in, choose a strategy, consider automated crypto trading and to store our cryptocurrency.

The critical knowledge to be imbibed in this chapter however, is to know how the pro traders insulate and bullet-proof themselves from getting burnt when a project goes up massively, either because of a news or a general market euphoria. Let us use The Sandbox project as a case in point to shed light on what to do when a coin suddenly explodes in value. In November of 2021 $SAND coin had just gone up fuelled by the market news on her $90 million fundraiser, plus, an incoming Alpha Pass Launch announcement. As soon as the news broke out, it led to $SAND exploding in value. If for instance, you bought 10,000 worth of $SAND at $0.50 and it shot up to $2.50, you will definitely be in outrageous profit. However, between the intervening hours when you go to sleep and wake up, anything can happen. The value, for instance, could go down to $0.80.

The critical question at this juncture is in the face of this bad news, how you can stop yourself from getting burnt. This is where you should use the sell orders and stop losses. You definitely should think like a pro in this situation. If the price goes downwards or a little below the price you bought, you should sell it all immediately. You should take the little percentage loss as a hit; in some cases, it is not very much, in others, it could be quite heavy. It is certainly a lot less than getting burnt and losing a quarter or more of its value. This will particularly come down hard on whale traders who have the mathematical possibility of losing six figures overnight in a matter of hours.

You certainly need to put in place security measures to prevent being burnt. What a pro trader does normally before bed time, is set an OCO (One Cancels the Other)) order in place. This terminology in essence means you set a stoploss and take-profit order. Some other crypto traders have other plans to prevent getting burnt. Sometimes the price can go down a bit and then really explode. If they sold all their coins when the price went down a bit, this would mean that they cannot benefit when the price goes right back up. To avoid losing out all together, they put a stop loss on a percentage of their holdings, which would help them achieve two things, firstly, if the price drops below their buy position, they can go ahead to double their portfolio with the percentage that was sold off. And if the price doesn't drop, then they are still in business. This strategy is applied mostly if your intentions are long term, plus, the project has huge growth potentials.

Some of these traders have different price range that they want to sell. So, they put an instruction to sell if it goes below a certain threshold. They can also sell incrementally just in case the price explodes again.

As you already know, cryptocurrency is composed of the trading aspect which is short term and the investment aspect which is long term. Even if you are involved in cryptocurrency for the long term, you obviously will not like to invest in a cryptocurrency that will ultimately lose value. But the price matters less if you are in it for the long haul because you definitely have a long way to go. It could possibly be for months or even years or even decades as the case may be. A Binance coin was once worth $3 but currently worth $600. It can easily go up to $1000 or $2000. Another example is Solana, in 2020 it was worth just below $3, but a year after (2021), it is now worth $200 and could easily reach $1000 in future.

Risk Management: The 2% Risk Per Trade Approach

Every trade you take comes with risk. There is no trader in the world that is able to make winning trades 100% of the time.

Fig. 7: Protecting Yourself from Getting Burnt is Everything

One of your main priorities as a trader is to practice proper risk management. This means managing your trades in such a way that even if a trade hits your Stop Loss multiple times in a row, you will still have enough capital to stay profitable.

An important method for managing risk is to adjust the amount of capital you use to enter a trade, also known as position sizing.

This does NOT mean placing your stop loss 2% away from your entry. Your entry price, take profit levels, and stop loss should all be determined by technical analysis. The 2% risk per trade strategy only helps you determine how much capital you should put into that particular trade.

For instance, if you have a $2000 account. Your risk per trade is calculated by getting 2% of $2000, which gives us a **Risk Per Trade of $20**

Now suppose you want to place a trade for an asset/coin which is currently trading at $10.Looking at the chart, you see some strong support at $9.20 and decide to place your **Stop Loss at $9.10**

Now let's calculate the risk per asset. For each XYZ asset you purchase, how much would you lose if the stop loss is hit? By calculating the difference between the entry level and stop loss level ($10 -$9.10), which will give us a RISK PER ASSET of $0.90

After calculating these numbers, you are now ready to determine how many coins you should buy for this trade.

Therefore, Risk Per Trade / Risk Per Asset/Coin = Amount of Assets to Buy

Risk Per Trade / Risk Per Coin = Number of Coins to Buy $20 (2% of $1000) / 0.90 (Entry – Stop Loss) = 22.22

You can now place your trade, buying 22.22 coins at $10 for $22.22

So, if price comes back down to $9.10 and your stop loss is hit, you will sell your 22.22 coins for $202.2, thereby bringing your loss to $20, which is 2% of your investment (capital) on that particular coin/token.

Please practice responsible trading and use 2% (or less!) risk for each trade you take to ensure that you never lose so much in one trade that you destroy your portfolio or lose your money

OFIT

This question is a recurring decimal, the reason and motivation for venturing into cryptocurrency business. People are constantly thinking of how to make enough income to take care of themselves, dependents and how to live the good life. People are definitely not in cryptocurrency trades or any human endeavour for play. The strides and moves made by traders are mainly driven by profit motives.

People involved in cryptocurrency trade are eager to turn their efforts into a profit-making operation and will certainly do whatever that is needed to become successful.

People in the crypto community are very interested in the best time to cash-in, to leave a trade and make huge gains. The truth is that you can actually develop the psychological reflex and understanding to know when to cash-in or leave for profit. You don't have to rely completely on other people's profit points to make your own. Get information from people, community and groups, but make an informed effort to decide your own profit points.

It is important that you study and understand the tactics of whale investors, the moves that have propelled them to the very top and sustained them there for years or even decades. Their pattern of behaviour which has made them successful include the following:

Daily 5-10% Gain and Exit

Cryptocurrency can go up to even 1000%. This happens on a daily basis. In the maze of this rollercoaster swings, you should constantly look out for consistency. Do not be taken in by this price swings. The way to go is to look for 5-10% daily and exit. This is what full-time traders do on daily basis. They make their money trading the same or different coins daily. They are not interested in those mouth-watering numbers. They invest large sums of money and make their 5-10% profit. This is certainly one of the most effective ways of building a retirement fund through trading cryptocurrencies.

News/Speculations

There are times when cryptocurrency really spikes in value. It is more than just the community being active or that people are speaking about it in one of the big cryptocurrency forums or that someone spoke about it in the news. This development actually affects the cryptocurrency. Updates can certainly enhance it. If it is in the news, for instance that they are creating a new wallet or finished product, or they have just a partnered with a fortune 500 company or the board is pivoting or adding something else to their product. In this category are the things that can constitute market news which has the capacity to initially drive-up demand for that cryptocurrency.

Speculation comes into the mix. News drives up the price and could also lead speculators to go into a trade speculatively. News and speculation work hand in hand. There is a marked difference between real news and speculative news.

The point to be made is that sometimes there is no news, just pure speculation but in these instances, you can make huge amount of profit. Bear in mind that this profit is temporary and not based on something significant happening to a cryptocurrency. In this case, you can make between 20-59% gain and then exit.

Trending Cryptocurrency

This is when you are anticipating a high and something else exploded and you get behind the next best cryptocurrency to the one that just spiked. In this instance, people will come to the conclusion that it is rather too late to get into the one that just boomed. They jump immediately to the one that is really cheap. This normally makes the price to explode. You should know that this is temporary or ad hoc and happens every now and then. There are definitely many ways of making a profit but you need to decide your own profit point. Don't rely too much on anybody else', think of your own.

How To Harness the Best Profit

It is of utmost importance that you develop acute knowledge and psychological balance on how to make the best profit in cryptocurrency and then deploy it to devastating effect. Nothing good comes easy and only a few things happen by accident. So, if you desire to make the best profit in cryptocurrency trading and investing, you need to make preparation for the profit. In as much as, it is imperative for one to feel the pulse of what is happening within the Crypto community, so you can buy into projects before their peak, you however, have to be careful not to jump on something during the peak, cos if you do, you definitely stand the risk of losing it altogether or making a very small profit.

You need to feel the pulse and be behind the Communities. This is one of the hardest things to do. Unfortunately, so many people that are in the trading and investing business are lazy and practically rely on other people to assist them to either trade or invest in cryptocurrency. This is not the mentality of a winner.

It's far better for you to prepare yourself and take the bull by the horns, have control of your business and not someone else. The truth is that, people are in the business for different reasons. For instance, you cannot really differentiate from the people that are trying to drive up demand for their coin and people who have some news. This is how you can be in control of your activities:

Join Communities

This includes joining Twitter, follow the major coins, newer coins and the ones that you are excited about. Join the Facebook groups related to cryptocurrency.

You should pay sufficient attention to understanding the pulse, what people are excited about, what have they heard. From the various groups that you belong to, it will be easy for you to know when something is about to pump. You need to also carry out your research to understand and quality-check the news/ information that you are receiving. If it is true, then you can ride the wave with them. Communities can really be beneficial because sometimes it benefits the members carrying the news to let you know that something is about to happen. This helps drive up the price.

Set up Alerts/ Google Search

A constant and consistent part of your profit preparation is to make sure that you check Google news regularly. Also, set up Alerts to your phone so that anytime any news drops from major cryptocurrency news sources, you will be in the know. Always check on Google. If something is happening within the community, people are saying a lot of things about a cryptocurrency, that it is surging in price, all you need to do is to do a Google search, quality check the information and then you can get behind it.

Have Money (USDT, BUSD, USD) Ready on Your Favourite Exchanges

It may sound counter intuitive but it is important that you have money ready. A lot of times, people want to keep their money in the wallet. This is fairly the standard practice. But because transferring from one exchange to the other can come with hassles and you can actually miss a trading opportunity if your money is not ready to trade on your favourite exchange. So, it is important for you to have some money ready. Because, if you have money ready and you see what the pulse is on, you can get straight to Investing.

Don't Risk More Than You Can Afford

If you overstretch yourself, go all out and invest, it could be devastating if you lose. You could end up owing people a lot of money and may even be forced to sell your prized assets in order to liquidate your debt. So, you should not risk more than you can afford. A lot of whale investors put six figures into one trade. tthat's a huge risk but if they lose it, they could probably roll with the punches and move on because they can afford it.

Be sure to Decide Your Out Point & Stop Loss

It is inevitable that you decide the price you will sell at. Once you have decided, stick with it and do not change your mind. If you see that something is really surging, you may be tempted to think that it could go by ten, fifteen, twenty per cent and then change your selling price. This could tank significantly and backfire and have your portfolio burnt. Do not become greedy or emotional. Make sure you have a Stop Loss in the background, in an event of a price swing, it automatically starts selling while you sleep. If you don't have stop loss, you could lose money.

CHAPTER

CRYPTO TECHNICAL ANALYSIS

Technical Analysis is a vital tool in the operations of many cryptocurrency traders. But it is important that you know that it doesn't tell you what will definitely happen.

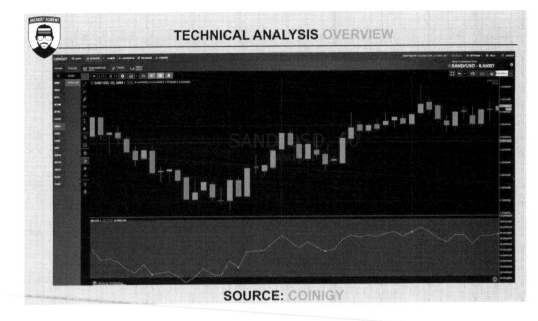

SOURCE: COINIGY

Fig. 8: Technical Analysis Overview

All it does is that it tells you what is likely to happen given the historical information analysed through the study of charts. However, for it to be effective, it requires to be done accurately.

By its very nature, technical analysis studies price movements through the use of charts. Adroit traders use technical analysis to make money from price movements. The major assumptions of Technical Analysis include:

- All available information is reflected in the price.

- Human psychology is repetitive

- Statistical analysis is critical and can help uncover the behaviour pattern of prices.

This section on Technical Analysis will give you the tools to put data and intelligence behind your trading decisions, to spot price movements of a cryptocurrency and be able to decide whether it is the right time to buy and/or to sell a cryptocurrency. Technical Analysis will arm you with data to enable you make the best decision. Technical Analysis is not 100% error free but most of the time, it helps traders arrive at the right decision.

To fully understand the dynamics of Technical Analysis, how it can help you become a sophisticated and successful cryptocurrency trader, it is important that you fully participate in the Cryptocurrency Training course www.nyceayuk.com. This on demand course is fully loaded and will transform you into the sophisticated crypto investor/ trader that you had always wanted to be

CHAPTER **11**

HOW TO REMAIN ON TOP OF THE TRADING GAME

Twitter

Twitter is one of the best sources of information on cryptocurrency. Given recent advancements, you can now follow cryptocurrency and be abreast of all the latest developments on Twitter. For instance, one of the members of the UTRUST ICO team went to Microsoft's Web Summit to talk about the future of online payments. This development is really a very important news in terms of driving up the value. The implication and reality are that the company is getting more exposure by being in the presence of and rubbing shoulders with powerful tech companies. With the aid of Twitter, you can really have a good understanding of what is happening with all the categories of cryptocurrency from ICOs to established cryptocurrencies. Through it, you can understand what is happening in the market. It is important that you follow a host of cryptocurrencies especially the ones that you are interested in understanding what is happening within the community, the team, what they are developing.

You can also follow a range of people within the cryptocurrency community. This will enable you get the most up-to-date information when it is released from the people themselves. It is certainly better for you to find out the most up-to-date information directly instead of waiting for other people to find out the information and then post on Facebook.

It is best for you to join Twitter and follow cryptocurrency coins, companies and influential people within the cryptocurrency world so that you can understand what is going on within the community. It is also advisable for you to follow YouTubers and people who are actively involved with the community. This will enhance your knowledgeability of a crypto asset; plus help you understand what is likely to pump soon.

Kryptocal.com

The desire of every crypto trader is to get news or information about projects on their upcoming events and more importantly announcements before the information hits the crypto community. KRYPTOCAL.COM is that ninja tool you need if you must be ahead of everyone else.

Cypherhunter.com

Cypherhunter is a global, open data library and curation application that helps blockchain and crypto trading enthusiast learn about the narrative, conversations and story associated with crypto assets. Ultimately, it is the data layer that allows you to get information about those (whales) backing or those (whales) who have invested in a crypto asset.

For example, if you get on cypherhunter.com and search for a crypto asset, in this instance BLOKTOPIA, you are going to see the following venture capitalists (VCs) and that including Polygon, Avalanche, Kucoin, AU21 and more as her investors. Now, with information like this and a metaverse project, I can almost guarantee your mind is made up on investing on BLOK and for the long haul, considering BLOK is just $0.04, and also it is currently listed on only 3 exchanges as at the time of writing this.

BlockFolio (FTX)

BlockFolio, now FTX is a mobile app that tracks a wide range of cryptocurrencies and allows you to monitor your holdings in one place. This simplifies the process of viewing your holdings and their value, especially in comparison to thousands of currencies that you do not hold. You can then make better decisions about buying and selling.

With the BlockFolio app you can easily make your assessment of cryptocurrencies and their value much simpler. With all your information in one place, you won't have to spend time logging into individual accounts to see your values or the financial state of your portfolio.

Use Social Media to Stay on Top of The News

The determination to stay on top of the cryptocurrency game is down to the steps that you take. One of the best decisions that you should take is to join as many communities as possible. This will help you understand what is happening in the market.

Breakout Academy's Club is a group you may consider joining as a member.

There are specific groups for a specific cryptocurrency routine. Your membership of a specific group will enable you gain understanding of what is happening with that particular cryptocurrency so that you can trade the news when it happens. It is also desirable that you join crypto asset groups, discussion groups, telegram and others that will enhance your knowledge and hopefully, help you slay at the very top of your trading game.

CONCLUSION

If after reading this book, you are substantially equipped with the knowledge and tools that you can use to dominate cryptocurrency trading, then the effort is worth it. I believe that the nuggets I have espoused here will inculcate in you, the acute sense to know when to buy at the right time and sell at the right time. This to me is the major preoccupation of the book.

GLOSSARY

Key Cryptocurrency Trading Terminologies

Trading – Acronyms

Low Time Frame (LTF) charts as applied to fast-moving markets like crypto and FX are typically defined as anything from a 1 minute to a 1hour chart.

Medium Time Frame (MTF) charts as applied to fast-moving markets like crypto and FX are typically defined as anything from a 4hour to a 12hour chart.

High Time Frame (HTF) charts as applied to fast-moving markets like crypto and FX are typically defined as anything from a 1 day to a 1month chart.

Price Action (PA) is the price movement plotted over time.

Order Blocks (OB) are used to identify high impact price levels in which heavy trading has occurred. They create support and resistance levels on charts, especially when occurring at the highs and lows of a trading range. They are helpful in determining entry and exit points.

Support/Resistance Flips (S/R Flip) occurs when price action turns key resistance levels into support or key support levels into resistance. They are used for entering or closing positions.

Trend Lines (TL) show up on most charts. They express themselves as boundaries which hold price within a certain range. We identify breakouts and trading opportunities when the trend lines are broken.

Breakout (BO) occurs when price crosses a key resistance or support level. These are used as signals to go long or short.

Stop Loss (SL) is used to limit losses from adverse price movements.

Take Profit (TP) levels for placing limit sell or trailing take profit orders.

Higher High (HH) is when the highest price of a new candle is greater than the highest price point – the price previously reached before moving down.

For example, if the price previously topped out at $100 before moving down, a higher high would be formed if a new candle closed above $100.

Higher highs combined with higher lows are usually associated with uptrends.

Higher highs combined with higher lows are usually associated with uptrends.

Lower High (LH) is when the highest price of a new candle is lower than the highest price points – the price previously reached before moving down.

For example, if the price previously topped out at $100 before moving down, a lower high would be formed if the price went back up but did not reach $100 before going back down. Lower highs combined with lower lows are usually associated with downtrends.

Lower Low (LL) is when the lowest price of a new candle is less than the lowest price points – the price previously reached before moving up.

For example, if the price previously went down and stopped at $80 before moving up, a lower low would be formed if price went back down and closed below $80.

Lower highs combined with lower lows are usually associated with downtrends.

Pullback (PB) is when the price reverses temporarily but does not move beyond the start of the trend/swing before continuing to move with the trend. In a bullish trend, pullbacks are typically an opportunity to buy, however, in a downtrend, they offer levels to exit or go short.

Some traders use pullback to refer only to temporary reversals in a downtrend, and throwback to refer to temporary reversals in an uptrend.

Throwback (TB) occurs when price breaks through a resistance level, then comes back down to retest the same level as support before continuing to move up.

Swing Failure Pattern (SFP) occurs when a trend comes to an end. This could be when price fails to make a new high following a series of higher highs and higher lows in an uptrend. In a downtrend, the SFP occurs when price fails to make a new low moving average or simple moving average (MA or SMA). Exponential Moving Average (EMA).

MA/EMA bull cross Occurs when the faster moving average crosses above the slower moving average. A common example of this is the 12 EMA crossing up through the 26 EMA.

MA/EMA bear cross Occurs when the faster moving average crosses below the slower moving average. One example would be if the 12 EMA crossed down through the 26 EMA.

Bollinger Bands (BB) consist of three lines in total. The middle band (also known as the basis line) is typically the 20-day SMA. The outside bands are generally 2 standard deviations +/- from the 20 SMA.

Bollinger Bands are a measure of price volatility, and approximately 90% of price action takes place between the upper and lower BB. They are used for multiple purposes, but the most significant price moves occur upon breakouts above or below the bands.

OSCILLATORS

Money Flow Index (MFI) uses price and volume to identify overbought/oversold conditions. It can also highlight divergences and warn of an incoming trend change.

On-Balance Volume (OBV) indicates momentum by using volume changes. OBV shows crowd sentiment, which can be predictive of a bullish or bearish outcome.

Relative Strength Index (RSI) compares recent bullish and bearish price momentum to show overbought/oversold conditions. It is commonly used to confirm overbought conditions when above 70% and oversold when below 30%.

Stochastic (Stoch) consists of a signal line and a base line. When the signal line crosses the base line, it shows a momentum flip. Traders may wait for this to occur before entering positions near the bottom.

Stoch reacts to momentum rather than absolute price and is also popular for indicating overbought/oversold conditions.

Stochastic RSI (Stoch RSI) applies the stochastic oscillator onto a set of RSI values rather than to standard price data. It utilizes both momentum indicators to create a more sensitive one that reflects historical performance rather than a general analysis of price change.

A Stoch RSI reading above 80% is considered overbought, while below 20% is considered oversold.

PRICE CLOUD

The *cloud* is a collection of technical indicators that show important levels of support/resistance as well as overall trend and momentum. When price is above the cloud, it is bullish. If price is below the cloud, it is bearish, and if it is inside the cloud, it is neutral.

Kijun-sen (KJ) line is the base line used in the Ichimoku cloud, and the mid-point of the 26-period high and low.

Tenkan-sen (TK) line is the conversion line used in the Ichimoku cloud, and the mid-point of the 9-period high and low.

The TK cross, when the Tenkan-sen crosses the Kijun-sen, this can be used to provide trading signals.

VOLUME OUTLOOK (VISIBLE RANGE)

The *volume profile* is a vertical histogram which displays the amount of trading activity that has historically taken place at any given price level within the visible range on a chart.

High Volume Nodes (HVN - mountain peaks) on the volume profile indicate value zones where the highest trading volumes have occurred. They are used as support/resistance levels that price will not easily break through.

Low Volume Nodes (LVN - valleys) on the volume profile are the opposite of HVNs. They are zones where price moves occur more rapidly but spend less time, due to being in an "unfair value area".

Typically, price moves toward an LVN following a breakout or breakdown of the proceeding price pattern.

ABOUT THE AUTHOR

Nyce Ayuk is an acclaimed serial entrepreneur, business coach, author and celebrated authority on Bitcoin and cryptocurrency. In his latest book, The Cycle of Bitcoin Profit, he unveils the techniques and strategies critical for creating wealth as Crypto traders and investors.

His acumen, vast experience and passion for creating something out of nothing finds full expression in this epochal work.

It is a table shaker that will set you on the path to irreversible success either as a Crypto trader or investor.

Never in the past decade has the keys to unlocking the secrets to wealth in the crypto ecosystem been so laid bare than now for those who crave wealth and financial success. It is unputdownable.

Printed in Great Britain
by Amazon